YOU KNOW ME
The Gita
HINDUISM

Translation and Introduction by

Irina N. Gajjar

Sanskrit Illuminations by

Navin J. Gajjar

Emerald Ink Publishing, Inc.
Houston, Texas

Published by:

Emerald Ink Publishing, Inc.
Houston, Texas 77075

800-324-5663
E-mail emerald@emeraldink.com
http://www.emeraldink.com

Printed and bound in the United States of America

Cover design by Leo Fortuno.
Book design by Brockton Brown.

ISBN 1-885373-27-9

Dedication

To Nilima, Anand, and Gopika

who inspired this work

and to

Devika and Ravi

who commented on it when it was finished.

Foreword

Dr. Irina Gajjar has presented the English speaking world with its first pristine translation of the Bhagavad Gita, or the Gita. The simplicity and beauty of her work distinguish it from the many existing versions which translate words instead of concepts or which strain to provide single explanations for ideas that lend themselves to multiple interpretations.

Irina became my mentor when I was fifteen years of age. She and her family provided me with academic guidance and inspiration and nurtured my philosophical needs by introducing me to the richness of Hinduism.

You Know Me is the fruit of many years of Sanskrit study and an extended effort to prepare a translation that enables young Hindus and persons unfamiliar with Hinduism to understand and appreciate the spiritual, practical, and philosophical tenets embodied in the Gita which is its essence.

The three discrete titles of this work represent the three levels upon which it may be read. First, ***You Know Me*** suggests that anyone with a pure heart, even a child, can understand God. Every reader or listener endowed with faith knows God and intuits the symbolism and truth in His words.

The second title, ***The Gita***, identifies the work as divinely inspired. In the Bhagavad Gita Lord Krishna gives answers to the questions and dilemmas of life and death. He explains and guides us toward the paths that lead to unity with God.

The third title, ***Hinduism***, states that the Bhagavad Gita crystallizes the vast body of philosophy, ethics, and spirituality of which this faith is comprised. This title is directed towards students, scholars and philosophers who have an interest in learning about Hinduism or in reconciling the paradoxes that characterize the Hindu way of life and thought: action and inaction, conflict and peace, one God and many divine manifestations, philosophy and mythology, reincarnation and nirvana.

In this millennium, few Hindus and even fewer people interested in Hinduism have read and understood the Gita in its entirety because existing translations have been difficult to follow. Now the panorama has changed. ***You Know Me*** is easily comprehensible and a pleasure to read. It is a must for Hindus, for persons who wish to understand Hindu values, and for philosophers who question the meaning of human existence in a universal context.

Dr. Stefan Thomke
Harvard University

Author's Preface

You Know Me
The Gita
Hinduism

Truth is clear, poetic and concise. These qualities define classic works of philosophy, mythology and religion which nourish the soul and the intellect. From this perspective, one of humanity's greatest classics is the Bhagavad Gita, or Gita, the Hindu gospel. In the Gita, God enables those with faith, symbolized by Arjun, to know Him and answers universal questions asked by believers, agnostics and philosophers. Since Sanskrit is a complex language, it can be difficult to preserve the essential clarity of the questions and answers in translation. ***You Know Me, The Gita, Hinduism*** is a simple yet accurate English language Gita which strives to capture this clarity.

I have purposefully kept my work free of commentary. It is written from the perspective of a linguist and a student of Hinduism, not as a theorist promoting a particular viewpoint. ***You Know Me*** is intended for people of all ages and levels of sophistication. The inconsistencies and ambiguities in the text exist in the Sanskrit and are left to the readers to analyze if they chose to do so. Terms which do not lend themselves to facile translation have been explained in a glossary so as not to interrupt the flow of the text.

Like the Sanskrit Gita, ***You Know Me*** is written in blank verse. To maintain the flow and rhythm in English, the verses do not always correlate. However, each English page on the right corresponds to the Sanskrit on the left.

Feminine and masculine pronouns have been used interchangeably as have the words man and woman. In the Sanskrit, the term "man" and the masculine are used generically to represent the human race. The mission of this work has been to reincarnate the Gita as an English work using English structure. Only in this way can the beauty, depth and logic of the Sanskrit original survive translation.

The words of God spoken in the Gita are placed in context through a brief introduction entitled "Origins." This section gives a concise history of the Bhagavad Gita and of the culture in which it was born and matured, a culture which it continues to dominate today with flexible strength.

You Know Me was conceptualized to address young readers, but after the work was completed, it became clear that no modification could make it more appropriate for a broader, more learned audience. I tried from the beginning to make this English Gita flawless and to avoid added complexity or artifice. Thus, I think it fills a void in the history of world literature and religion.

Irina Gajjar

Contents

Origins

The exact age of the Bhagavad Gita is not known. Some scholars and religious teachers insist that the Gita is more than five thousand years old, but more probably it dates to about 500 B.C., which makes it about 2,500 years old. Thus, it has existed in people's thoughts for at least thirty-five lifetimes. Whatever its age, this text is among the most beautiful and inspiring works of philosophy ever created by the human race.

The words "Bhagavad Gita" translate into English as "Song of God." The word "Gita" was used to describe systems of philosophy and the word "Bhagvan" means God. The Bhagavad Gita guides the lives and outlook of Hindus today as it has since its creation. There are over seven hundred million Hindus in the world, mostly in India, who believe that the Gita synthesizes the meaning of life and faith. Nevertheless, there are considerable differences in the interpretation of its message. Because the work is open-ended and allows its readers to focus on their own truth, its followers are free to disagree about specifics. For example, the Bhagavad Gita describes three paths to achieving enlightenment and immortality: knowledge, devotion and action. Religious preachers debate as to which path is the preferred one and they cite different passages to support their particular position.

The Gita is written in Sanskrit, a complex and sophisticated language which expresses elaborate thoughts succinctly and with simplicity. Sanskrit is viewed not merely as a language, but also as an extension of philosophy and it has always been studied by scholars from this perspective.

The Bhagavad Gita comes from a chain of thought going back at least to India's Vedic period, which began about 1500 B.C. Although not many details are known about the development of Indian philosophy before the Vedic period, archaeologists have uncovered a great deal of information about life and customs in India, as far back as approximately 6,000 B.C. It is known that the beginning of animal husbandry and the reaping of wild and cultivated wheat was already established in this period. From these simple societies, ancient Indian people developed full fledged urban economies in the third millenium B.C.

Notably, the emergence of early Indian civilizations coincided with that of the Sumerian city-states of ancient Mesopotamia. There are divergent theories as to how such monumental change came about at different places at about the same time. That these distinct cultures were in touch with one another is evidenced by the presence of reciprocal and related artifacts excavated at various sites. Other information suggests the existence of navigation as well as overland travel early on. However, scholars are divided between the theory that the centrally located West Asian societies contributed to the development of ancient Indian civilizations and the theory that the two cultural units developed as a result of indigenous evolution. These theories can be reconciled by the view that the ancient cultures of the Fertile Crescent and Northwest India evolved from a common source but that they matured differently in response to different socio-economic stimuli.

Human skeletons and skulls of different races were uncovered at early Indian sites. Although the finds are not conclusive, the divergence supports the view of some Western ancestry and the existence of international trade. Most of the skeletons were of a mediterranean type called Dravidian. The Indians of today are mainly a mixture of Dravidians and Aryans, with the Dravidian traits more prominent in the South.

The ancient Indian civilization which flourished approximately between 2,500 B.C. and 1500 B.C. is called the Indus Valley or Harappan Civilization because its artifacts were first excavated at Harappa and Mohenjodaro. Subsequently, many other sites have been studied which indicate that Indus Valley communities were fairly widespread through the Northwest regions of India and Pakistan. This civilization coexisted with Mesopotamian civilization, as mentioned above, and with the Helladic and Minoan civilizations of Greece and Crete, respectively. There is also evidence of similarities in the decorative designs found in the Indus Valley and in both Greece and Crete. Many examples of like motifs have been found in artifacts, particularly pottery. Female figurines with exaggerated hour glass torsos, which apparently represented mother goddesses, were common to ancient India, Mesopotamia, and Crete. The nature of the similarities and the items excavated again indicate common roots as well as commercial interaction.

Ancient Indian cities of this proto-historic age were well planned with brick houses several stories high and good drainage systems. They also had public baths, which perhaps were of ritualistic significance. Construction bricks were made in standard sizes of 40 X 20 X 10 centimeters or 30 X 15 X 7.5 centimeters, all with the ratio of 4: 2: 1. This precision demonstrates a good knowledge of arithmetic. From the excavations, we know that the people who built these cities played games including hopscotch and marbles, made attractive toys, and apparently wore draped garments not unlike the "dhotis" worn by men in India today.

By far the most intriguing discoveries are the seals and other items bearing inscriptions which reputable scholars have been struggling to decipher for over half a century. Notwithstanding much ongoing analysis, comparison, and speculation, we have not yet even been able to establish definitively whether this mysterious script is alphabetic or pictographic.

The decline of the Indus Valley civilization is associated with the beginning of the Vedic period which gave birth to Hinduism as we know it today. During that period, between about 1500 B.C. and 600 B.C., people known as Aryans came from Northwest Asia across the mountains and spread into India. Their movements have been traced through their pottery known as "painted grey ware." Aryans spoke a language that was of Indo-European origin. That means it had the same roots as the languages of North India and Europe. In India this language developed into Sanskrit. Modern North Indian languages like Hindi and Sindhi come from Sanskrit, much as the romance languages like Spanish and French come from Latin.

The Aryans had different physical characteristics and were lighter in complexion than India's native Dravidians. They were mobile and good fighters. The two peoples battled and ultimately the Aryan newcomers won. The Aryans changed North India considerably; in the South, the Dravidians were able to preserve more of their old customs and to maintain their very different languages.

Originally nomads, the Aryans settled down after some time in houses made of wood and bamboo, much like some of the homes built in Indian villages and suburbs today. Families were close, like today's families. Marriage was a sacred bond and the extended family of sisters, brothers, and cousins was the foundation of society. Groups of families formed a clan, groups of clans formed a district, and several districts formed a tribe. The tribes came to be governed by a king.

Eventually society organized itself into an inflexible hierarchical system based on occupations, known as the caste system. It became virtually impossible to change one's position and nature of occupation or to marry someone from a caste different from that of one's birth. The four castes were Brahmins, or priests, Kshatriyas, or warriors, Vaisyas, people working in the trades or agriculture and the lower classes, or Sudras (Shudras). Within this broad hierarchy, there were sub-castes which further determined social status. The caste system lingers as an attitude in modern day India, even though the Indian Constitution forbids discrimination based on caste. This system formerly defined Hindu society, but it also created injustices not unlike injustices experienced by minority groups in the United States.

Most of what we know about the Aryans comes from the Vedas, their sacred literature, as the physical finds of the Vedic period were not as impressive or abundant as those of earlier times. The original literature was undoubtedly an oral tradition long before it was written. It was passed on by word of mouth from generation to generation. By 500 B.C. the Vedas and Vedic thought were well established in India. However, not all the writings have been preserved or studied. Interestingly, the earliest surviving Sanskrit manuscripts have not been found in India itself, but rather to the North in Central Asia and Western China; they are Buddhist, not Hindu texts.

"Veda" means knowing. The Vedas are not any particular work, but are the vast body of literature which talks about holy knowledge. The Vedas are divided into three groups: collections of hymns and prayers, the Samhitas; writings about the meaning of the hymns and prayers called Brahmanas; and the Upanishads which are meditations or thoughts about God, the world, and the human soul. The Upanishads are partly combined with the Brahmanas.

The fundamentals of Hinduism can be traced back to the Vedas. Many ideas in the Bhagavad Gita can be identified in Vedic literature, though in less developed form. Some examples are the concept of divine worship and the ideas of karma and reincarnation.

Historians consider the Vedic period to have ended about 600 B.C. At this time India was divided into some sixteen or more independent states. Most were ruled by kings, but some had constitutions and were ruled by the people or by oligarchies. As in other places, the kingdoms were occasionally united by marriages between the royal families while at other times they were divided by wars. At one point, about 500 B.C., Persia extended its rule over parts of India. Later (about 327 B.C.) the Macedonian Emperor, Alexander the Great, defeated several Indian kingdoms in vigorous battles. But after two years he was forced to retreat, leaving an artistic tradition as his main legacy.

Life for the affluent in ancient India was luxurious. Writings describe beautiful homes, furniture, and lavish clothes and jewels. The houses had gardens with birds, flowers and swings. People socialized, bathed daily and enjoyed perfumes and incense. They ate a variety of foods including vegetables, fruits, milk products, meat, fish, wheat and rice. Although there was preaching against it, some drank liquor. For entertainment there was music, dancing, dramas, poetry, story telling, games, sports and gambling.

The end of the Vedic period was marked by the emergence of

new ideas about God, happiness and the human spirit. Four important new religions developed. Two of these religions, Buddhism and Jainism, marked a break with orthodox Hinduism. The other two, Vaishnavism and Saivism (Shaivism), were more of a reform from within.

All these creeds survive today. Buddhism is no longer a major religion in India, but from its birthplace there it spread throughout the Far East. It is also a dominant religion in Sri Lanka, the island of Ceylon, which was formerly a part of India. In India, Buddhism was a major religion for several centuries. However, the Indian Buddhists eventually lost royal support and readopted Hinduism. The great philosopher Sankaracharya (788 - 820 A.D.) reconverted many Buddhists to Hinduism, using debates as a means of preaching. Jainism didn't spread abroad, but it continues to be very strong in parts of India today. Vaishnavism and Saivism are still encompassed by mainstream Hinduism.

Originally Buddhism focused on salvation rather than worship, but after Budda's death in about 486 B.C., He himself came to be worshipped as God. Lord Buddha taught that it was futile to speculate about God because it is impossible to learn or know about Him with certainty. Buddha's goal was to help people avoid suffering by teaching them to live according to four Noble Truths and the Eightfold Path. The truths are that the world is full of suffering; that desire and attachment are the causes of worldly life; that worldly life can be stopped if we destroy desire and attachment; and that to do this we must learn the way. The way is the Eightfold Path: right speech; right action; right living; right effort; right thinking; right meditation; right hopes and right view. The Eightfold Path leads us to "Nirvana," a state of eternal bliss and peace.

Jainism similarly centered on conduct rather than devotion, although its teachers were and continue to be deeply revered. Jainism was founded by Vardhamana Mahavira, the last of twenty-four important teachers called Tirthankaras. Mahavira, meaning great hero, lived from about 540 B.C. to 468 B.C. The point of Jainism is to become free from the fetters of both pleasure and pain by means of self control and penance. Mahavira taught five great commandments which lead to the truth. Four commandments came from earlier teachings: tell the truth; own no property; do not hurt anything living; and do not accept anything which is not free. The fifth commandment which was added by Mahavira is to observe chastity.

Mahavira preached that owning nothing should be taken literally, so he got rid of everything he had, including his clothes. He spent the last thirty years of his life unclothed. The Jains later divided into two groups, those who believe that monks should be virtually naked, and those who do not. Many Jains do penance by fasting regularly for days without even water. In order not to hurt any living thing, strict Jains strain their water so as not to drink any small insect by mistake. They eat before dark, so no bugs fall in their food. Jains are pure vegetarians and do not eat anything which is dug up from the ground, like potatoes, because when you dig something up, you kill insects in the earth. Notwithstanding these restrictions, the Jain diet is varied and nourishing.

Although Buddhist and Jain thought were offsprings of Hinduism, these religions underwent substantial change, unlike Vaishnavism, originally called Bhagavatism, and Saivism which preserved their Vedic roots. Bhagavatism is part of the Bhagavad Gita. In the beginning, Bhagavatism introduced the idea of one God and taught that loving worship was better than sacrificing animals or performing other ritualistic ceremonies. Later this faith developed into Vaishnavism, the worship of God in the form of Lord Krishna.

Saivism, the worship of Lord Siva (Shiva), originated in part in the appeasement of Rudra who represented the scary, destructive powers of nature in the Vedas. People believed that Rudra's anger caused disasters and diseases and they thought that he could be kept happy and quiet with gifts and prayers. Rudra merged into Siva, the supreme God who was the soul of the world, the creator and the protector. Siva, or a form of Siva, is also believed to have been a religious figure in the Indus Valley Civilization because of representations which are reminiscent of His more recent forms. Siva can be seen by the heart, not by the eyes. The force of Siva is vividly sensed in the Gita when Krishna transforms Himself to display God's awesome power.

The Bhagavad Gita itself is a part of the Mahabharata, one of India's two great Epics; the other is the Ramayana. These tales came into being after the Vedic age. While the Vedas represent the perspective of the Brahmins, or priestly classes, the Epics generally reflect the viewpoint of the warriors and other classes. They are less esoteric and are filled with exciting adventures. Some ideas and symbolism in the Mahabharata and Ramayana also appear to be derived from earlier, pre-Vedic, Indian beliefs.

The Epics depict life and values in ancient India and dramatically illustrate the prevailing mores. People admired family love, faithfulness, truth and strength while they disdained treachery, faithlessness, and cowardice. Much of what is described is universal, but some customs, for example polyandry, are more specifically related to aspects of the ancient social structure. The Mahabharata and Ramayana were completed over a long period of about six or eight hundred years, by the third or fourth century A.D. The stories were disseminated as an oral tradition and were expanded, elaborated, and fine tuned as people told them over and over. Today in India we see large canvases, which cover entire walls, depicting intricate narratives. These canvases were a basis for story telling and it is probable that travelling story tellers in the past used similar pictures to develop the tales in the Epics.

The Ramayana is the story of Lord Rama, a prince who was forced to go and live in the forest for fourteen years because his stepmother wanted her own son to inherit the kingdom. Rama 's brother Bharat left Rama's sandals on the throne as a symbol that he would return; Rama's father, the King, died of a broken heart. Sita, Rama's wife, and Lakshman, another brother, went with Rama. But the demon Ravana stole Sita and took her away to the island of Ceylon. Rama and his allies fought hard and finally rescued Sita. The couple then returned, becoming King and Queen and the parents of twin sons. However, after some time, the public questioned Sita's purity because she had been Ravana's prisoner. They demanded that Sita walk through fire to prove that she had remained true to Rama. Sita was so hurt that she no longer wished to be Queen, so, after proving her faithfulness, she disappeared into the earth, her mother.

The Mahabharata is more complex than the Ramayana. It branches out into many side stories about morality, politics, and religion. The Bhagavad Gita is one such side story. Overall, the Mahabharata describes a great war between two branches of the royal family called the Bharatas. The word Bharat today is the Indian word for India. The Mahabharata means the Great Bharat, or the great story of the Bharatas.

In the 1980s both the Mahabharata and the Ramayana were produced as long elaborate TV serials which were shown in one hour segments every Sunday morning all over India. Each serial lasted for about a year. Almost everybody in India watched these stories simultaneously. While the serials were being shown, the streets were virtually empty and all activity came to a standstill.

Most Indians have always had a general idea about the Mahabharata and the Ramayana, but today all the details are very well and widely known. Video tapes of the Epics are available in India and abroad and they are watched over and over. The videos thrill, entertain and educate young and old from all walks of life.

In the first millennium A.D., as Hinduism matured, Indian politics and culture developed and India continued to have ongoing relations with the outside world. Roman seafarers traded with South India and early Christian missionaries came to preach. Buddhist pilgrims came from China to visit and study the birthplace of Buddhism. In about 500 A.D. the Huns, who invaded the Roman Empire, also created problems in India. Meanwhile the kings who ruled in different states struggled for power. By about 800 A.D. there were three great powers: the Palas, the Gurjara-Pratiharas, and the Rashtrakutas. Their conflicts as well as other struggles weakened India and left the door open for foreign invasion.

During this period, powerful Muslim states to the west of India became aggressive and they spread far and wide, further west to Europe and East to India. In Europe, knights fought crusades against them. The Muslims swept over and conquered Spain in only seven years (between about 707 A.D. and 714 A.D.) and it took over seven centuries to fully defeat them. The last Muslim stronghold in the south, Granada, was overtaken by Spanish Christians in about 1492, the same time Columbus discovered America.

In India, between about 997 A.D. and 1150 A.D., vigorous Muslim armies won victory after victory. By the end of this period Muslim kingdoms controlled almost all of North India. Unlike Spain, India did not oust the Muslims. Even after the partition of India and the creation of the Muslim nation of Pakistan (originally West and East Pakistan, now Pakistan and Bangladesh) following independence from England in 1947, many Muslims chose to remain in India itself.

Although the Hindus did not vanquish Muslim kingdoms, ongoing battles flared among rulers and among people. Once again constant fighting weakened India and this time it was the British who were able to gain power. The British originally came to India to trade. They were looking for gold and spices, just as Christopher Columbus, who at first thought America was India. However, beginning in about 1750, the British became involved in Indian politics and they gradually gained power in many states. A big mutiny in 1857 temporarily shook them up, but the British regrouped and stayed in control. They followed a policy of divide and conquer and added fuel to the fire of Hindu-Muslim fighting. It wasn't until two centuries later, after the Second World War, that India won its independence from the British.

As in America and Africa, British rule left a permanent legacy in India. Educated Indians learned English and became familiar with English ways. English imperialism in India coincided with the beginning of the Industrial Revolution in England and with the spread of industrialization to the rest of the world. The Industrial Revolution marked the beginning of modern times and this coincidence has led to confusion in India between westernization and modernization. Even today some people mistakenly believe that modern educated Indians who speak fluent English, travel and are comfortable with American or European clothes and food are westernized.

In reality, India has had ongoing connections with Western culture from proto-historic times. The early Dravidians of the Indus Valley Civilization clearly had contacts with the West. The Aryans came from the West. Then the Muslims spread Indian learning to Spain and the rest of the world and brought new ideas to India from the West. In 1498, the famous Portuguese explorer Vasco da Gama sailed to India and established a Portuguese and Catholic foothold in Goa, on the coast not too far from Bombay. Finally, the English came and by the time they left, travel and communication all over the world was becoming easier. In many ways modern life has brought the whole world even closer together.

As we venture into the new millenium, the information age is accelerating communication with the United States and other countries. Furthermore, large numbers of American and other nationals of Indian origin routinely travel back and forth between India, the land of their roots, and their new homelands. These people, known in India as NRIs (Non-Resident Indians), regularly transport ideas, customs, technology and value systems as well as material objects like food, clothes and household goods.

Yet, notwithstanding the quickening pace of international interaction, in profound and substantial ways, India and Hinduism have not changed since the time of the formulation of the Bhagavad Gita. The beliefs of today are the same as the beliefs of 500 B.C. In many respects Hindus and Indians still live the same way they lived then. In ancient times people listened to story tellers dramatize the Mahabharata and the Ramayana. Today they watch them on television. But the stories are the same and the viewers still identify with the heroes, fear the villains and wrestle with the age old issues of power, love, and religious faith.

The Hindu way of life has developed over the centuries, but in essence it has not changed since the Gita was written. People's habits and customs remain fundamentally unaltered. Joint or extended families continue to be a basic way of life. People live with their parents and their brothers' families under one roof. Many times, even if families live separately, they share money. Indians feel responsibility for their entire extended family, not just for themselves and their children. Of course this is not always true, but it is the ideal and the norm. Indian traditions are based on respect for elders and ancestors and on close involvement in the affairs of family and good friends.

Hindu beliefs play an important role in people's daily lives because they are intertwined with everything people do and think. Although Hinduism is a philosophy composed of ideas and beliefs which can differ significantly from person to person, the philosophy determines individual or family behavior such as vegetarianism, daily worship or meditation. The Gita presents the opportunity for each individual to think about life, death, God, goodness, and destiny in her or his own way. Yet it also sets forth certain clear underlying principles. It is not necessary to believe any of these principles in order to be a Hindu, but most Hindus believe them.

Perhaps the most important underlying idea in Hinduism is that life's goal is to know the Truth. Knowing the Truth is an all encompassing concept. It is really everything: the essence of immortality, liberation and bliss. The Gita explains that Truth can be attained by learning, worship and action. Related to this concept, is the combined notion of karma and reincarnation. Hindu philosophy presumes that it is impossible to complete one's destiny in a single lifetime. Karma, meaning destiny which is neither random nor arbitrary, and reincarnation are the answer to the human question of why things happen as they do. We know from science that physical phenomena result from cause and effect. If we drop a glass, it will break. If we see a broken glass on the floor, we know from experience that it fell or was dropped. We know precisely what caused the glass to break, even if we didn't see how the glass got broken. In the same way Hindus believe that if something happens in this life, it was caused by something which happened before, either earlier in this life, or in an earlier life, even if they cannot remember the earlier life or event. Not remembering is analogous to not seeing the glass break.

Believing in karma and reincarnation is like believing that what goes around, comes around, although perhaps not in one lifetime. Some Hindus do not categorically believe in reincarnation as an empirical reality, but they consider this hypothesis to be the most plausible explanation for the mysteries of life and death as well as a lodestar which guides their conduct.

Because Hindus believe that God has countless appearances or manifestations, most non-Indians do not realize that Hindus worship only One God who has no form. A Divine appearance can be imagined and nevertheless be real because it is real in the mind. This belief explains the awesome physical descriptions of God in the Bhagavad Gita. It also explains the presence of photographs and statues of God in many different forms in Hindu homes and temples. Of course not all the representations portray God; some depict other characters or creatures from the epics or other legends. Sometimes we see various symbols of God and God's power; but Hindus know that the real spirit of God is invisible except in the mind's eye or the heart's eye.

One pleasant aspect of Hinduism is that people usually worship God in their own homes which are the primary center of religious activity. Occasionally some may go to a nearby temple or perhaps on a pilgrimage to a distant temple, but these excursions are generally for an outing or to satisfy a promise or vow. Many homes have a little temple room or a temple niche in a corner of a room. From time to time, a family decides to have a ceremony, called a "puja," at home and arrangements are made for the family priest to come and officiate. The family prepares flowers, fruit and sweets for the ceremony. The sweets are offered to God and then distributed and eaten as holy food.

Often friends are invited to come and watch. The ceremony lasts a couple of hours and everyone generally enjoys themselves. Sometimes, if the puja goes on too long, it becomes somewhat tiresome, but then people feel virtuous about displaying patience. On occasion they simply tell the priest to hurry the ceremony along.

There are many different kinds of ceremonies which have their origins in Vedic rituals. Some are connected with holidays, like Diwali, the festival of lights and the Hindu New Year. At New Year offerings are made to Lakshmi, the goddess of wealth. Other ceremonies are connected with important events in peoples' lives such as marriage, the birth of a child, ground breaking, or moving into a new home. Some pujas are held to ask God for assistance or to thank God for something good that has transpired.

During the ceremony the participants sit cross legged and the priest explains what is going on in the local vernacular language as he chants or reads in Sanskrit. He asks the participants to perform symbolic acts like bathing or feeding a small image of God. At the end, a tiny fire is lit in a tray and the tray is passed around. People put their hands above the holy fire, called Arthi, and then they put them on their eyes to get holy light or enlightenment, which is knowledge of the Truth.

In its totality, Hinduism is as much a philosophy and a way of life as it is a religion. It can accommodate individualism and change without losing its definition or power. Its roots are in Aryan traditions as adapted to the earlier culture of the Indus Valley civilization. Hinduism has endured because of its strength and flexibility. The ideas enunciated in the Bhagavad Gita can be interpreted in endless ways and yet remain consistent. Thus, these ideas are the impetus behind Hinduism as well as a reflection of its essence, ancient yet forever fresh.

India's wisdom is like the ocean into which many rivers flow. The waters in the ocean are always changing, but the ocean stays the same. Sometimes it storms, and other times it is calm; sometimes its waters are clear and other times they are opaque. Sometimes it expands and floods the beaches; other times it recedes. Still the ocean remains unchanged.

Prelude

The Mahabharata

The Mahabharata is the story of a great war fought in ancient India between princes who were cousins. It is a story of India's past, and like all great tales, it lives on in the present in the minds and hearts of the people of today.

The exciting deeds of kings and princes, queens and princesses, of gods and goddesses as well as of demons and other creatures fill the pages of this grand epic. Many fine heroes shine through their courage and strength. But among all these heroes, Arjun was perhaps the greatest because it was to him that, in the Bhagadvad Gita, the Lord revealed the truth about life and death and about God Himself.

Arjun and his four brothers, Yudishtir, Bhim, Nakul, and Sahadev were called the Pandavas, because they were sons of King Pandu of Hastinapura. They were born in the forest after King Pandu, who had become sick, left his throne. The Pandavas were not ordinary children. They were gifted by the gods, and were said to have been born gleaming with heavenly light.

When King Pandu died, his sons were still young so they returned with Kunti, their mother, to Hastinapura, where they found their cousin Duryodhana ruling. Duryodhana, son of the blind King Dhritarashtra, was the eldest of the hundred Kauravas and he was fiercely jealous of the Pandavas, especially of all the praises showered upon them by the people of Hastinapura. Thus, though Duryodhana and the Kauravas pretended to welcome the Pandavas, they secretly plotted their ruin.

In an atmosphere of hidden fear and distrust, the Pandavas grew up to become fine strong men. They were well educated as Kshatryas, or warriors, in the arts of peace as well as of war and they managed to keep safe and to protect themselves from Duryodhana's plots. They escaped from a burning building and won Draupadi, a Panchala princess as their bride. The five Pandava brothers all shared Draupadi as their wife.

Finally the Kauravas, advised by the wise older men in the court, agreed to make peace with the Pandavas and gave them a small, empty piece of land to rule, thinking they would not prosper there. However Yudishtir, who became king, was wise and strong and he soon turned this land into a rich and happy kingdom. He built a wonderful new city, Indraprastha, which he made his capital. The Pandavas became so rich and strong that King Yudishtir was able to perform the Rajasuya sacrifice which proved him to be the most powerful and greatest ruler in the country.

Yudishtir and his brothers naturally invited the Kauravas to the Rajasuya sacrifice and the celebration which followed, and Duryodhana stayed on at Indraprastha for some time as his cousins' guest. But the more Duryodhana saw of the Pandavas' greatness and wealth, the more his jealousy and anger grew and the more he determined to see the Pandavas destroyed.

At last Duryodhana made a plan and managed to get the consent of his blind aged father, King Dhritarashtra. He decided to get

King Yudishtir to agree to play a game of dice. Duryodhana's plan was to cheat in the game and to make King Yudishtir gamble away his kingdom.

Yudishtir received Duryodhana's invitation with doubts. He didn't trust Duryodhana and he knew that gambling was not a good thing; but yet he loved it and felt sure he would win. He also thought it would not be polite or honorable to refuse and so Yudishtir accepted the challenge. On the day of the game, the Pandavas entered the new gambling hall that had been especially built for this match. Drona, the teacher and Bhim, the great wise uncle of both the Kauravas and the Pandavas, and others sat with the blind Dhritarashtra and watched in silence and with heavy hearts.

The game began. Yudishtir staked a pearl necklace. He placed it on the board and lost it. He staked his jewels and lost them. He staked the gold and silver in his kingdom and lost that too. He staked and lost his chariots, elephants, horses and cattle. He lost his slaves and lost all he had and yet he would not stop until he lost his kingdom, his freedom and the freedom of his brothers. Finally losing all self control he staked his wife, Draupadi, and lost her as well.

Dhritarashtra perceived before him the dishonored Draupadi and his conscience could not bear the burden of her misery. So the old King tried to calm her and promised to grant whatever she might wish. Draupadi asked only that she and the Pandavas be freed and that her husbands be given their weapons. Dhritarashtra granted these requests. He begged the Pandavas' forgiveness for Duryodhana's deeds and begged them to accept the return of Indraprashta. In this way the Pandavas set off for home.

When Duryodhana heard what his father had done, he became

furious. He sent for the Pandavas again, and challenged them to one final game of dice. Yudishtir, even after all that had happened, would not refuse although his brothers begged him to. So the five brothers returned to Hastinapura. The final game was a strange one. The loser would go into the forest for twelve years and would spend a thirteenth year hiding in disguise. Should he be discovered, he would have to spend twelve more years in the forest.

Yudishtir agreed. He played again and lost. So the Pandavas with Draupadi went into the wilderness and Duryodhana ruled their kingdom.

Time passed and the thirteenth year of the Pandavas' exile came. The brothers decided to spend it in Matsya working in the court of King Virata. Their plan succeeded and neither the Pandavas nor Draupadi were discovered. But when the Pandavas made themselves known, the Kauravas refused to return their kingdom. Duryodhana refused to give them any land at all; he refused even as much land as would cover the point of a needle.

In this way the Kauravas set the stage for war. The Pandavas had no choice and they made preparations. Warriors from other kingdoms took sides. Many didn't know what to do because they were related to both the Kauravas and the Pandavas, but at last everything was decided. Both the Kauravas and the Pandavas asked for Lord Krishna's help. Krishna agreed to give his whole army to one side and to give himself as charioteer to the other. Duryodhana selected the army and Yudishtir's brother, Arjun, chose Lord Krishna to be his chariot driver. There was no turning back. Everything was ready and the day of the battle dawned.

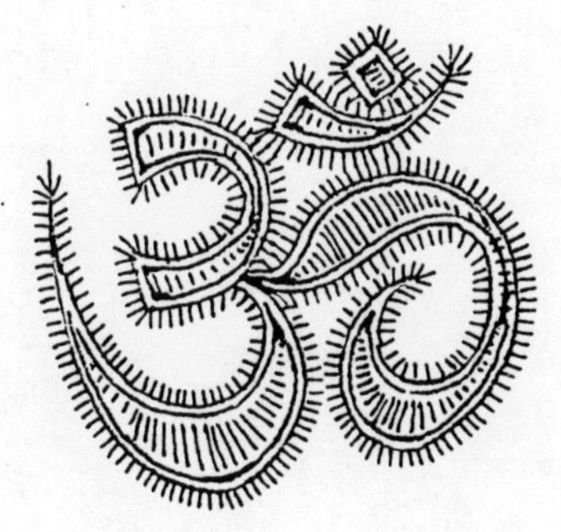

As Arjun sat in his chariot, watching his army and the army of his enemy
his mind started spinning.
He saw his great wise uncle Bhishma, his teacher Drona,
the hundred Kauravas who were his cousins,
and he felt he could not make himself fight them.

King Dhritarashtra was blind. But God
gave divine magic eyes to his minister, Sanjay.
With these divine eyes, Sanjay could watch the Great Mahabharata War.
Sanjay could watch from the royal palace and describe everything that
happened on the battlefield,
even though neither of them was there.

श्रीपरमात्मने नमः

अथ श्रीमद्भगवद्गीता

प्रथमोऽध्यायः

धृतराष्ट्र उवाच
धर्मक्षेत्रे कुरुक्षेत्रे समवेता युयुत्सवः ।
मामकाः पाण्डवाश्चैव किमकुर्वत सञ्जय ॥ १॥

Chapter 1

Arjun's Sadness

King Dhritarashtra asked Sanjay:

Oh Sanjay, what did my sons,

the Kauravas, and the sons of my brother

Pandu, the Pandavas, do standing on

the holy field of Kurukshetra all

ready and anxious to fight each other?

सञ्जय उवाच

दृष्ट्वा तु पाण्डवानीकं व्यूढं दुर्योधनस्तदा ।
आचार्यमुपसङ्गम्य राजा वचनमब्रवीत् ॥ २ ॥
पश्यैतां पाण्डुपुत्राणामाचार्य महतीं चमूम् ।
व्यूढां द्रुपदपुत्रेण तव शिष्येण धीमता ॥ ३ ॥
अत्र शूरा महेष्वासा भीमार्जुनसमा युधि ।
युयुधानो विराटश्च द्रुपदश्च महारथः ॥ ४ ॥
धृष्टकेतुश्चेकितानः काशिराजश्च वीर्यवान् ।
पुरुजित्कुन्तिभोजश्च शैब्यश्च नरपुङ्गवः ॥ ५ ॥
युधामन्युश्च विक्रान्त उत्तमौजाश्च वीर्यवान् ।
सौभद्रो द्रौपदेयाश्च सर्व एव महारथाः ॥ ६ ॥
अस्माकं तु विशिष्टा ये तान्निबोध द्विजोत्तम ।
नायका मम सैन्यस्य संज्ञार्थं तान्ब्रवीमि ते ॥ ७ ॥
भवान्भीष्मश्च कर्णश्च कृपश्च समितिंजयः ।
अश्वत्थामा विकर्णश्च सौमदत्तिर्जयद्रथः ॥ ८ ॥
अन्ये च बहवः शूरा मदर्थे त्यक्तजीविताः ।
नानाशस्त्रप्रहरणाः सर्वे युद्धविशारदाः ॥ ९ ॥
अपर्याप्तं तदस्माकं बलं भीष्माभिरक्षितम् ।
पर्याप्तं त्विदमेतेषां बलं भीमाभिरक्षितम् ॥ १० ॥
अयनेषु च सर्वेषु यथाभागमवस्थिताः ।
भीष्ममेवाभिरक्षन्तु भवन्तः सर्व एव हि ॥ ११ ॥
तस्य सञ्जनयन्हर्षं कुरुवृद्धः पितामहः ।
सिंहनादं विनद्योच्चैः शङ्खं दध्मौ प्रतापवान् ॥ १२ ॥

Sanjay answered:

When the Pandavas' army was all ready,

your son, Prince Duryodhana,

saw them and said:

The mighty army of the Pandavas is prepared!

It is strong. But in our own army

there are heroes just as brave as the Pandavas.

Our own heroes are just as

strong as Bhim and Arjun.

Our army is unconquerable.

Then the glorious old uncle Bhishma

roared like a lion and

blew on his conch to cheer

Prince Duryodhana on.

Then conches, drums and trumpets blared

forth and there was a great noise.

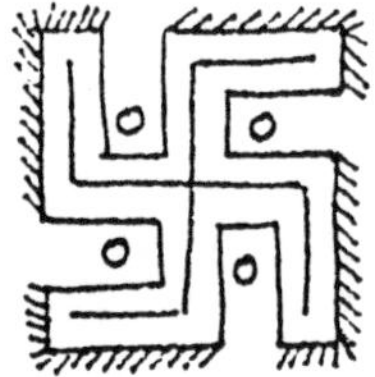

ततः शङ्खाश्च भेर्यश्च पणवानकगोमुखाः ।
सहसैवाभ्यहन्यन्त स शब्दस्तुमुलोऽभवत् ॥१३॥
ततः श्वेतैर्हयैर्युक्ते महति स्यन्दने स्थितौ ।
माधवः पाण्डवश्चैव दिव्यौ शङ्खौ प्रदध्मतुः ॥१४॥
पाञ्चजन्यं हृषीकेशो देवदत्तं धनंजयः ।
पौण्ड्रं दध्मौ महाशङ्खं भीमकर्मा वृकोदरः ॥१५॥
अनन्तविजयं राजा कुन्तीपुत्रो युधिष्ठिरः ।
नकुलः सहदेवश्च सुघोषमणिपुष्पकौ ॥१६॥
काश्यश्च परमेष्वासः शिखण्डी च महारथः ।
धृष्टद्युम्नो विराटश्च सात्यकिश्चापराजितः ॥१७॥
द्रुपदो द्रौपदेयाश्च सर्वशः पृथिवीपते ।
सौभद्रश्च महाबाहुः शङ्खान्दध्मुः पृथक्पृथक् ॥१८॥
स घोषो धार्तराष्ट्राणां हृदयानि व्यदारयत् ।
नभश्च पृथिवीं चैव तुमुलो व्यनुनादयन् ॥१९॥

Then Arjun of the Pandavas blew
on his heavenly conch in reply.
Arjun sat in a glorious chariot
pulled by white horses.
Lord Krishna himself was Arjun's charioteer.

Lord Krishna also blew a conch;
Bhim did too.
King Yudishtir, Nakul, and Sahadev
all blew their conches as well.

And there was a terrible sound
echoing through heaven and earth
and it tore the hearts of Dritarashtra's sons,
the Kauravas,
and made them afraid.

अथ व्यवस्थितान्दृष्ट्वा धार्तराष्ट्रान्कपिध्वजः ।
प्रवृत्ते शस्त्रसंपाते धनुरुद्यम्य पाण्डवः ॥२०॥
हृषीकेशं तदा वाक्यमिदमाह महीपते ।
सेनयोरुभयोर्मध्ये रथं स्थापय मेऽच्युत ॥२१॥
यावदेतान्निरीक्षेऽहं योद्धुकामानवस्थितान् ।
कैर्मया सह योद्धव्यमस्मिन् रणसमुद्यमे ॥२२॥
योत्स्यमानानवेक्षेऽहं य एतेऽत्र समागताः ।
धार्तराष्ट्रस्य दुर्बुद्धेर्युद्धे प्रियचिकीर्षवः ॥२३॥
एवमुक्तो हृषीकेशो गुडाकेशेन भारत ।
सेनयोरुभयोर्मध्ये स्थापयित्वा रथोत्तमम् ॥२४॥
भीष्मद्रोणप्रमुखतः सर्वेषां च महीक्षिताम् ।
उवाच पार्थ पश्यैतान्समवेतान्कुरूनिति ॥२५॥
तत्रापश्यत्स्थितान्पार्थः पितॄनथ पितामहान्
आचार्यान्मातुलान्भ्रातॄन्पुत्रान्पौत्रान्सखींस्तथा ॥२६॥
श्वशुरान्सुहृदश्चैव सेनयोरुभयोरपि ।
तान्समीक्ष्य स कौन्तेयः सर्वान्बन्धूनवस्थितान् ॥२७॥
कृपया परयाविष्टो विषीदन्निदमब्रवीत् ।
दृष्ट्वेमं स्वजनं कृष्ण युयुत्सुं समुपस्थितम् ॥२८॥

At this moment, Arjun, Pandu's son,
lifted up his bow
and spoke to Lord Krishna
saying:

Lord Krishna, place my chariot between the two armies.
Keep it there until I have seen
all the warriors and decided against whom to fight.

Then Sanjay continued:
Arjun saw both armies.
He saw in both armies
his uncles and teachers and cousins
and brothers and sons and grandsons and friends.
Seeing all his relations ready
to fight against him, he felt very sorry and sad.

सीदन्ति मम गात्राणि मुखं च परिशुष्यति ।
वेपथुश्च शरीरे मे रोमहर्षश्च जायते ॥२९॥
गाण्डीवं स्रंसते हस्तात्त्वक्चैव परिदह्यते ।
न च शक्नोम्यवस्थातुं भ्रमतीव च मे मनः ॥३०॥
निमित्तानि च पश्यामि विपरीतानि केशवः ।
न च श्रेयोऽनुपश्यामि हत्वा स्वजनमाहवे ॥३१॥
न काङ्क्षे विजयं कृष्ण न च राज्यं सुखानि च ।
किं नो राज्येन गोविन्द किं भोगैर्जीवितेन वा ॥३२॥
येषामर्थे काङ्क्षितं नो राज्यं भोगाः सुखानि च ।
त इमेऽवस्थिता युद्धे प्राणांस्त्यक्त्वा धनानि च ॥३३॥
आचार्याः पितरः पुत्रास्तथैव च पितामहाः ।
मातुलाः श्वशुराः पौत्राः श्यालाः संबंधिनस्तथा ॥३४॥
एतान्न हन्तुमिच्छामि घ्नतोऽपि मधुसूदन ।
अपि त्रैलोक्यराज्यस्य हेतोः किं नु महीकृते ॥३५॥

In his sadness Arjun said to Lord Krishna:
Oh Krishna, I see my relations here ready
to fight and my legs shake.
My mouth is dry.
My hair is standing on end.
My bow is dropping out of my hand.
My skin is burning.
My mind is spinning. I cannot stand up.

And I cannot see any use in this war.
What is the use of killing my relatives in battle?

Oh Krishna, I do not want victory,
or a kingdom or pleasures.
What use are these three things?

Oh Krishna, I do not want to kill my relatives
even though they may kill me.

निहत्य धार्तराष्ट्रान्नः का प्रीतिः स्याज्जनार्दन ।
पापमेवाश्रयेदस्मान्हत्वैतानाततायिनः ॥३६॥
तस्मान्नार्हा वयं हन्तुं धार्तराष्ट्रान्स्वबान्धवान् ।
स्वजनं हि कथं हत्वा सुखिनः स्याम माधव ॥३७॥
यद्यप्येते न पश्यन्ति लोभोपहतचेतसः ।
कुलक्षयकृतं दोषं मित्रद्रोहे च पातकम् ॥३८॥
कथं न ज्ञेयमस्माभिः पापादस्मान्निवर्तितुम् ।
कुलक्षयकृतं दोषं प्रपश्यद्भिर्जनार्दन ॥३९॥
कुलक्षये प्रणश्यन्ति कुलधर्माः सनातनाः ।
धर्मे नष्टे कुलं कृत्स्नमधर्मोऽभिभवत्युत ॥४०॥
अधर्माभिभवात्कृष्ण प्रदुष्यन्ति कुलस्त्रियः ।
स्त्रीषु दुष्टासु वार्ष्णेय जायते वर्णसंकरः ॥४१॥
संकरो नरकायैव कुलघ्नानां कुलस्य च ।
पतन्ति पितरो ह्येषां लुप्तपिंडोदकक्रियाः ॥४२॥
दोषैरेतैः कुलघ्नानां वर्णसंकरकारकैः ।
उत्साद्यन्ते जातिधर्माः कुलधर्माश्च शाश्वताः ॥४३॥
उत्सन्नकुलधर्माणां मनुष्याणां जनार्दन ।
नरकेऽनियतं वासो भवतीत्यनुशुश्रुम ॥४४॥

Oh Krishna, what joy can there be in killing
Dhritarashtra's sons?
They are my family.
Only sin can come to us from killing.
It is wrong to kill Kauravas.
They are our cousins.
How can we ever be happy again
after killing our own relations?

Even if they do not understand this, we do.
We know that it is a sin to kill our own family.
Our family will be ruined.
Our women will become bad.
Our caste will become mixed.
Our race will be destroyed.
It would be better for me
if I let Dhritarashtra's sons kill me.

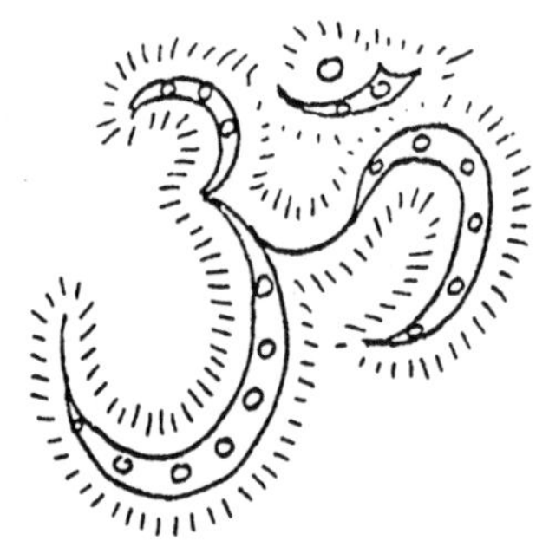

अहो बत महत्पापं कर्तुं व्यवसिता वयम् ।
यद्राज्यसुखलोभेन हन्तुं स्वजनमुद्यताः ॥४५॥

यदि मामप्रतीकारमशस्त्रं शस्त्रपाणयः ।
धार्तराष्ट्रा रणे हन्युस्तन्मे क्षेमतरं भवेत् ॥४६॥

एवमुक्त्वार्जुनः संख्ये रथोपस्थ उपाविशत् ।
विसृज्य सशरं चापं शोकसंविग्नमानसः ॥४७॥

Sanjay said:

Arjun spoke those words on the battlefield.

His mind was full of sorrow.

He put down his bow and arrows

and sat down sadly

in the back corner of his chariot.

श्री

द्वितीयोऽध्यायः

तं तथा कृपयाविष्टमश्रुपूर्णाकुलेक्षणम् ।
विषीदन्तमिदं वाक्यमुवाच मधुसूदनः ॥ १ ॥

कुतस्त्वा कश्मलमिदं विषमे समुपस्थितम् ।
अनार्यजुष्टमस्वर्ग्यमकीर्तिकरमर्जुन ॥ २ ॥

क्लैब्यं मा स्म गमः पार्थ नैतत्त्वय्युपपद्यते ।
क्षुद्रं हृदयदौर्बल्यं त्यक्त्वोत्तिष्ठ परंतप ॥ ३ ॥

Chapter 2

God Answers Arjun

Sanjay said:

Then Lord Krishna talked to Arjun who was
sad and full of pity.
Arjun's eyes were filled with tears.

Bhagvan said:

Arjun, how can you be so silly now?
You will be laughed at by everyone.
You will not go to heaven
and you will not be famous.
Do not be unmanly. It does not suit you.
Don't be weak. Be brave.
Rise and conquer your enemies!

कथं भीष्ममहं संख्ये द्रोणं च मधुसूदन ।
इषुभिः प्रतियोत्स्यामि पूजार्हावरिसूदन ॥ ४ ॥

गुरूनहत्वा हि महानुभावान्
श्रेयो भोक्तुं भैक्ष्यमपीह लोके ।
हत्वार्थकामांस्तु गुरूनिहैव
भुञ्जीय भोगान्रुधिरप्रदिग्धान् ॥ ५ ॥

न चैतद्विद्मः कतरन्नो गरीयो
यद्वा जयेम यदि वा नो जयेयुः ।
यानेव हत्वा न जिजीविषाम-
स्तेऽवस्थिताः प्रमुखे धार्तराष्ट्राः ॥ ६ ॥

Arjun said:

How, Krishna, can I fight Bhishma

and Drona with arrows on the battlefield?

I respect them.

It is better to live as a beggar,

but without killing,

because after killing them

our hands will be stained with their red blood.

We do not know what to do.

To fight or not to fight.

We do not know

if it would be better for us to win

or to lose and be conquered.

The sons of Dhritarashtra,

the Kauravas, are lined up against us

and we do not want to stay alive

by killing them.

कार्पण्यदोषोपहतस्वभावः
पृच्छामि त्वां धर्मसंमूढचेताः ।
यच्छ्रेयः स्यान्निश्चितं ब्रूहि तन्मे
शिष्यस्तेऽहं शाधि मां त्वां प्रपन्नम् ॥ ७ ॥

न हि प्रपश्यामि ममापनुद्याद्
यच्छोकमुच्छोषणमिन्द्रियाणाम् ।
अवाप्य भूमावसपत्नमृद्धं
राज्यं सुराणामपि चाधिपत्यम् ॥ ८ ॥

एवमुक्त्वा हृषीकेशं गुडाकेशः परंतप ।
न योत्स्य इति गोविन्दमुक्त्वा तूष्णीं बभूव ह ॥ ९ ॥

तमुवाच हृषीकेशः प्रहसन्निव भारत ।
सेनयोरुभयोर्मध्ये विषीदन्तमिदं वचः ॥ १० ॥

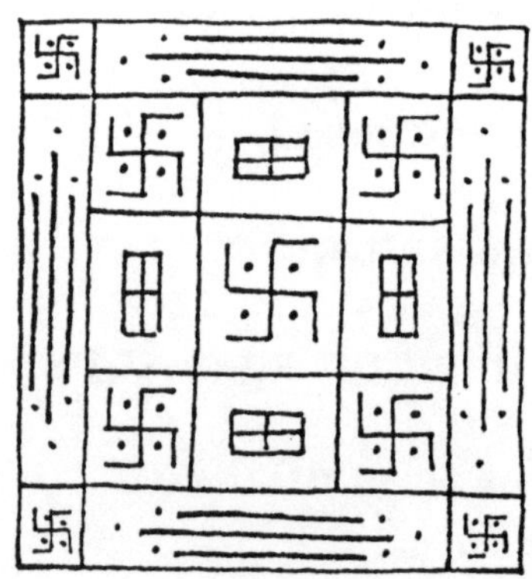

I am confused.
I do not know what to do.
I do not know what my duty is.
I pray to you,
tell me clearly
what is right and good for me.
Sadness is drying up my mouth.

Sanjay spoke to Dhritarashtra:
Oh King, after saying this,
Arjun told Lord Krishna a second time,
"I will not fight"
and then he kept quiet.

So Lord Krishna, smiling,
spoke to sad Arjun
who was still standing
in the middle of two armies.

अशोच्यानन्वशोचस्त्वं प्रज्ञावादांश्च भाषसे ।
गतासूनगतासूंश्च नानुशोचन्ति पण्डिताः ॥११॥
न त्वेवाहं जातु नासं न त्वं नेमे जनाधिपाः ।
न चैव न भविष्यामः सर्वे वयमतः परम् ॥१२॥
देहिनोऽस्मिन्यथा देहे कौमारं यौवनं जरा ।
तथा देहान्तरप्राप्तिर्धीरस्तत्र न मुह्यति ॥१३॥

Bhagvan said:

You pity those whom you should not pity.
Wise men do not pity those who are dead
nor those who are alive.
The reason is simple.

I, God, have always lived.
You and those Kings you pity
have always lived too.
And all of us will never stop living.

The soul of the little boy,
the young man, and the old man
does not change
even though the body changes.
And even if the soul moves
on to another body after the body dies,
the soul stays the same.

मात्रास्पर्शास्तु कौन्तेयः शीतोष्णसुखदुःखदाः ।
आगमापायिनोऽनित्यास्तांस्तितिक्षस्व भारत ॥१४॥
यं हि न व्यथयन्त्येते पुरुषं पुरुषर्षभ ।
समदुःखसुखं धीरं सोऽमृतत्वाय कल्पते ॥१५॥
नासतो विद्यते भावो नाभावो विद्यते सतः ।
उभयोरपि दृष्टोऽन्तस्त्वनयोस्तत्त्वदर्शिभिः ॥१६॥
अविनाशी तु तद्विद्धि येन सर्वमिदं ततम् ।
विनाशमव्ययस्यास्य न कश्चित्कर्तुमर्हति ॥१७॥
अन्तवन्त इमे देहा नित्यस्योक्ताः शरीरिणः ।
अनाशिनोऽप्रमेयस्य तस्माद्युध्यस्व भारत ॥१८॥
य एनं वेत्ति हन्तारं यश्चैनं मन्यते हतम् ।
उभौ तौ न विजानीतो नायं हन्ति न हन्यते ॥१९॥

So you see, you do not have to feel sad at all.
You cannot kill someone else's soul
and someone else's soul cannot kill you.
And the body doesn't matter.
Do not worry about killing the body.

Oh Arjun, do not worry about the body at all.
A wise person does not care about heat and cold
or about pleasure and pain.
These things belong to the body.
They come and go.
They are not permanent and so they are not real.

Only the soul is real.
And the soul can never be killed.
A wise person understands this.
For this reason, Arjun,
go and fight!

न जायते म्रियते वा कदाचिन्
नायं भूत्वा भविता वा न भूयः ।
अजो नित्यः शाश्वतोऽयं पुराणो
न हन्यते हन्यमाने शरीरे ॥२०॥
वेदाविनाशिनं नित्यं य एनमजमव्ययम् ।
कथं स पुरुषः पार्थ कं घातयति हन्ति कम् ॥२१॥
वासांसि जीर्णानि यथा विहाय
नवानि गृह्णाति नरोऽपराणि ।
तथा शरीराणि विहाय जीर्णा-
न्यन्यानि संयाति नवानि देही ॥२२॥
नैनं छिन्दन्ति शस्त्राणि नैनं दहति पावकः ।
न चैनं क्लेदयन्त्यापो न शोषयति मारुतः ॥२३॥
अच्छेद्योऽयमदाह्योऽयमक्लेद्योऽशोष्य एव च ।
नित्यः सर्वगतः स्थाणुरचलोऽयं सनातनः ॥२४॥
अव्यक्तोऽयमचिन्त्योऽयमविकार्योऽयमुच्यते ।
तस्मादेवं विदित्वैनं नानुशोचितुमर्हसि ॥२५॥

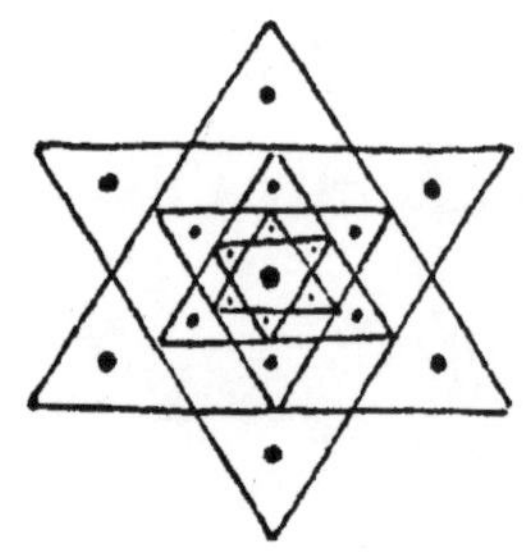

The soul is never born. It never dies.
It does not have a beginning
and so it has no end.
It is everlasting and immovable.

As a man takes off old clothes
and changes them for new ones,
so the soul removes its old body
and replaces it by a new one.

The soul cannot be cut by knives
or burned by fire, or wet by water,
or dried by the wind.

The soul cannot be seen nor described
nor imagined. The soul never changes.
It has no form, but it is everywhere.
So do not worry about the soul.

॥ ॐ ॐ ॐ ॐ ॥

अथ चैनं नित्यजातं नित्यं वा मन्यसे मृतम् ।
तथापि त्वं महाबाहो नैवं शोचितुमर्हसि ॥२६॥
जातस्य हि ध्रुवो मृत्युर्ध्रुवं जन्म मृतस्य च ।
तस्मादपरिहार्येऽर्थे न त्वं शोचितुमर्हसि ॥२७॥
अव्यक्तादीनि भूतानि व्यक्तमध्यानि भारत ।
अव्यक्तनिधनान्येव तत्र का परिदेवना ॥२८॥

आश्चर्यवत्पश्यति कश्चिदेन-
माश्चर्यवद्वदति तथैव चान्यः ।
आश्चर्यवच्चैनमन्यः शृणोति
श्रुत्वाप्येनं वेद न चैव कश्चित् ॥२९॥

देही नित्यमवध्योऽयं देहे सर्वस्य भारत ।
तस्मात्सर्वाणि भूतानि न त्वं शोचितुमर्हसि ॥३०॥

Oh Arjun, birth leads to death and death leads to birth,
so do not grieve over something that cannot be helped.
Everyone died before he was born
and was born before he died.
So what is there to be sad about?

All creatures are formless before birth
and formless after death.
They only have form during life
which is between birth and death.

Some see that the soul is wonderful;
some people say that the soul is wonderful,
and some hear that the soul is wonderful.
Yet some, even hearing, do not know the soul.

The soul which lives in the body cannot be hurt
or destroyed, so do not worry about it.

स्वधर्ममपि चावेक्ष्य न विकम्पितुमर्हसि ।
धर्म्याद्धि युद्धाच्छ्रेयोऽन्यत्क्षत्रियस्य न विद्यते ॥३१॥
यदृच्छया चोपपन्नं स्वर्गद्वारमपावृतम् ।
सुखिनः क्षत्रियाः पार्थ लभन्ते युद्धमीदृशम् ॥३२॥
अथ चेत्त्वमिमं धर्म्यं संग्रामं न करिष्यसि ।
ततः स्वधर्मं कीर्तिं च हित्वा पापमवाप्स्यसि ॥३३॥
अकीर्तिं चापि भूतानि कथयिष्यन्ति तेऽव्ययाम् ।
संभावितस्य चाकीर्तिर्मरणादतिरिच्यते ॥३४॥
भयाद्रणादुपरतं मंस्यन्ते त्वां महारथाः ।
येषां च त्वं बहुमतो भूत्वा यास्यसि लाघवम् ॥३५॥
अवाच्यवादांश्च बहून्वदिष्यन्ति तवाहिताः ।
निन्दन्तस्तव सामर्थ्यं ततो दुःखतरं नु किम् ॥३६॥

Besides, you have to think of your duty.
You are a Kshatriya, a warrior,
and to fight a war for a good reason
is your duty.

You are lucky to have the chance to fight in this war
for your duty will take you to God.
And if you do not fight,
you will be giving up your duty.
Giving up a duty is a sin.

People will laugh at you.
You will be ashamed.
The shame will be worse than death.
People will think you were afraid to fight.
Your enemies will say shameful things about you.

हतो वा प्राप्स्यसि स्वर्गं जित्वा वा भोक्ष्यसे महीम् ।
तस्मादुत्तिष्ठ कौन्तेय युद्धाय कृतनिश्चयः ॥३७॥
सुखदुःखे समे कृत्वा लाभालाभौ जयाजयौ ।
ततो युद्धाय युज्यस्व नैवं पापमवाप्स्यसि ॥३८॥
एषा तेऽभिहिता सांख्ये बुद्धिर्योगे त्विमां शृणु ।
बुद्ध्या युक्तो यया पार्थ कर्मबन्धं प्रहास्यसि ॥३९॥
नेहाभिक्रमनाशोऽस्ति प्रत्यवायो न विद्यते ।
स्वल्पमप्यस्य धर्मस्य त्रायते महतो भयात् ॥४०॥
व्यवसायात्मिका बुद्धिरेकेह कुरुनन्दन ।
बहुशाखा ह्यनंताश्च बुद्धयोऽव्यवसायिनाम् ॥४१॥
यामिमां पुष्पितां वाचं प्रवदन्त्यविपश्चितः ।
वेदवादरताः पार्थ नान्यदस्तीति वादिनः ॥४२॥
कामात्मानः स्वर्गपरा जन्मकर्मफलप्रदाम् ।
क्रियाविशेषबहुलां भोगैश्वर्यगतिं प्रति ॥४३॥
भोगैश्वर्यप्रसक्तानां तयापहृतचेतसाम् ।
व्यवसायात्मिका बुद्धिः समाधौ न विधीयते ॥४४॥

But if you fight,
you will either go to heaven or win victory.
So, Arjun, arise.
Make up your mind to fight.
Fight and do not worry about how the war turns out.
Do not care if you win or lose.
Do not care if your fighting brings pleasure or pain,
victory or defeat.
Just do your duty.
In this way you will be free.

If you are not worried about winning or losing,
about killing or being killed,
you will be able to do your duty very well
because you will not be afraid.
Your mind will be on your duty
and not scattered here and there.

त्रैगुण्यविषया वेदा निस्त्रैगुण्यो भवार्जुन ।
निर्द्वन्द्वो नित्यसत्त्वस्थो निर्योगक्षेम आत्मवान् ॥४५॥
यावानर्थ उदपाने सर्वतः संप्लुतोदके ।
तावान्सर्वेषु वेदेषु ब्राह्मणस्य विजानतः ॥४६॥
कर्मण्येवाधिकारस्ते मा फलेषु कदाचन ।
मा कर्मफलहेतुर्भूर्मा ते संगोऽस्त्वकर्मणि ॥४७॥
योगस्थः कुरु कर्माणि संगं त्यक्त्वा धनञ्जय ।
सिद्ध्यसिद्ध्योः समो भूत्वा समत्वं योग उच्यते ॥४८॥
दूरेण ह्यवरं कर्म बुद्धियोगाद्धनञ्जय ।
बुद्धौ शरणमन्विच्छ कृपणाः फलहेतवः ॥४९॥
बुद्धियुक्तो जहातीह उभे सुकृतदुष्कृते ।
तस्माद्योगाय युज्यस्व योगः कर्मसु कौशलम् ॥५०॥
कर्मजं बुद्धियुक्ता हि फलं त्यक्त्वा मनीषिणः ।
जन्मबन्धविनिर्मुक्ताः पदं गच्छन्त्यनामयम् ॥५१॥
यदा ते मोहकलिलं बुद्धिर्व्यतितरिष्यति ।
तदा गन्तासि निर्वेदं श्रोतव्यस्य श्रुतस्य च ॥५२॥
श्रुतिविप्रतिपन्ना ते यदा स्थास्यति निश्चला ।
समाधावचला बुद्धिस्तदा योगमवाप्स्यसि ॥५३॥
स्थितप्रज्ञस्य का भाषा समाधिस्थस्य केशव ।
स्थितधीः किं प्रभाषेत किमासीत व्रजेत किम् ॥५४॥

Oh Arjun,
do not care about opposites
like pleasure and pain.
Just work.
Do not care how your work turns out.
Do your work well.
This is being wise
and being wise takes you to God.
Being wise, you will not be confused.
Your mind will concentrate on God.

Then Arjun asked:
Oh Krishna,
how can we recognize a wise man
whose mind is concentrating
steadily on God?
How does a wise man speak, and sit and walk?

प्रजहाति यदा कामान्सर्वान्पार्थ मनोगतान् ।
आत्मन्येवात्मना तुष्टः स्थितप्रज्ञस्तदोच्यते ॥५५॥
दुःखेष्वनुद्विग्नमनाः सुखेषु विगतस्पृहः ।
वीतरागभयक्रोधः स्थितधीर्मुनिरुच्यते ॥५६॥
यः सर्वत्रानभिस्नेहस्तत्तत्प्राप्य शुभाशुभम् ।
नाभिनन्दति न द्वेष्टि तस्य प्रज्ञा प्रतिष्ठिता ॥५७॥
यदा संहरते चायं कूर्मोऽङ्गानीव सर्वशः ।
इन्द्रियाणीन्द्रियार्थेभ्यस्तस्य प्रज्ञा प्रतिष्ठिता ॥५८॥
विषया विनिवर्तन्ते निराहारस्य देहिनः ।
रसवर्जं रसोऽप्यस्य परं दृष्ट्वा निवर्तते ॥५९॥
यततो ह्यपि कौन्तेय पुरुषस्य विपश्चितः ।
इन्द्रियाणि प्रमाथीनि हरन्ति प्रसभं मनः ॥६०॥
तानि सर्वाणि संयम्य युक्त आसीत मत्परः ।
वशे हि यस्येन्द्रियाणि तस्य प्रज्ञा प्रतिष्ठिता ॥६१॥

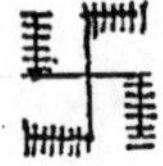

Bhagvan answered:

A wise man is he who is always satisfied

because he wants nothing.

He is happy by himself, inside himself

within his soul.

Because he is always satisfied,

the wise man neither feels joyful when he gets

something good, nor sad when he gets something bad.

He has no hate or envy. He is not afraid.

He is not angry. His mind is always calm.

A wise man is he who tries to control

his mind and senses. This means he tries

to separate himself from outside objects,

even though this is very difficult.

Yet a wise man always controls his mind

and concentrates on Me.

ध्यायतो विषयान्पुंसः संगस्तेषूपजायते ।
संगात्संजायते कामः कामात्क्रोधोऽभिजायते ॥६२॥
क्रोधाद्भवति संमोहः संमोहात्स्मृतिविभ्रमः ।
स्मृतिभ्रंशाद् बुद्धिनाशो बुद्धिनाशात्प्रणश्यति ॥६३॥
रागद्वेषवियुक्तैस्तु विषयानिन्द्रियैश्चरन् ।
आत्मवश्यैर्विधेयात्मा प्रसादमधिगच्छति ॥६४॥
प्रसादे सर्वदुःखानां हानिरस्योपजायते ।
प्रसन्नचेतसो ह्याशु बुद्धिः पर्यवतिष्ठते ॥६५॥
नास्ति बुद्धिरयुक्तस्य न चायुक्तस्य भावना ।
न चाभावयतः शान्तिरशान्तस्य कुतः सुखम् ॥६६॥

By thinking of objects, a person starts to want them.
And a person who always wants things
cannot have them all.
Then she gets disappointed.
Her disappointment makes her angry.
Her anger confuses her.
She loses her mind and is ruined.
She has no peace.

But a person who stops wanting things
is free from attachment.
She is free from loving things and free from hate.
Such a person is on the path that leads to peace.

How can a person without self control have peace?
And without peace,
how can she have happiness?

इन्द्रियाणां हि चरतां यन्मनोऽनुविधीयते ।
तदस्य हरति प्रज्ञां वायुर्नावमिवाम्भसि ॥६७॥
तस्माद्यस्य महाबाहो निगृहीतानि सर्वशः ।
इन्द्रियाणीन्द्रियार्थेभ्यस्तस्य प्रज्ञा प्रतिष्ठिता ॥६८॥
या निशा सर्वभूतानां तस्यां जागर्ति संयमी ।
यस्यां जाग्रति भूतानि सा निशा पश्यतो मुनेः ॥६९॥
आपूर्यमाणमचलप्रतिष्ठं
समुद्रमापः प्रविशन्ति यद्वत् ।
तद्वत्कामा यं प्रविशन्ति सर्वे
स शान्तिमाप्नोति न कामकामी ॥७०॥
विहाय कामान्यः सर्वान्पुमांश्चरति निःस्पृहः ।
निर्ममो निरहंकारः स शान्तिमधिगच्छति ॥७१॥

A person whose mind wanders
is like a lost boat on the water
carried here and there
by the wind.

But a person who has self control is calm and happy.
She is never sad.
She goes right inside God.

The wise woman who is part of God
sees beyond night and day.

Like the ocean stays calm
when rivers flow into it,
so a person with self control stays calm
no matter what flows into her mind.

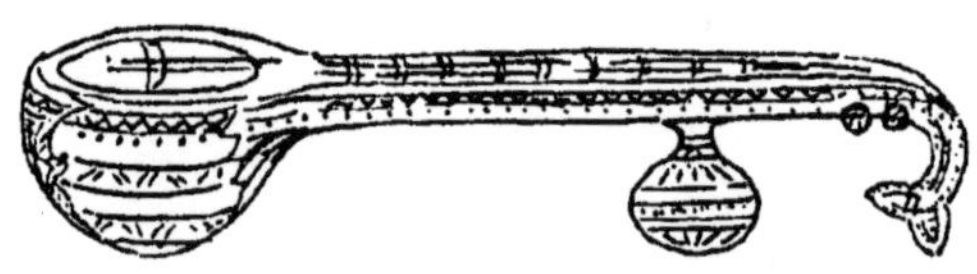

एषा ब्राह्मी स्थितिः पार्थ नैनां प्राप्य विमुह्यति ।
स्थित्वाऽस्यामन्तकालेऽपि ब्रह्म निर्वाणमृच्छति ॥७२॥

Oh Arjun,

you can easily

recognize the wise man

who is one with God.

He is at peace.

He understands truth.

He is calm

and he is forever happy.

श्री

तृतीयोऽध्यायः

ज्यायसी चेत्कर्मणस्ते मता बुद्धिर्जनार्दन ।
तत्किं कर्मणि घोरे मां नियोजयसि केशव ॥ १ ॥
व्यामिश्रेणेव वाक्येन बुद्धिं मोहयसीव मे ।
तदेकं वद निश्चित्य येन श्रेयोऽहमाप्नुयाम् ॥ २ ॥

Chapter 3

God Explains Right Action

Arjun asked Bhagvan:

Oh Krishna, if the wisdom of knowing truth

is even better than good action,

then why are you telling me to do this awful thing?

Why are you telling me to fight and kill?

You are mixing me up. Oh God,

please tell me clearly

the one way I can reach You.

लोकेऽस्मिन्द्विविधा निष्ठा पुरा प्रोक्ता मयानघ ।
ज्ञानयोगेन सांख्यानां कर्मयोगेन योगिनाम् ॥ ३ ॥
न कर्मणामनारम्भान्नैष्कर्म्यं पुरुषोऽश्नुते ।
न च संन्यसनादेव सिद्धिं समधिगच्छति ॥ ४ ॥
न हि कश्चित्क्षणमपि जातु तिष्ठत्यकर्मकृत् ।
कार्यते ह्यवशः कर्म सर्वः प्रकृतिजैर्गुणैः ॥ ५ ॥
कर्मेन्द्रियाणि संयम्य य आस्ते मनसा स्मरन् ।
इन्द्रियार्थान्विमूढात्मा मिथ्याचारः स उच्यते ॥ ६ ॥

Bhagvan answered:
Arjun, earlier I told of
two ways to reach God,
the way of knowledge
which is wisdom
and the way of action
which is doing your duty.

A person cannot ever really give up action
because a person cannot stop doing things,
not completely, even for a minute.
Our body forces us to do things.
A person who pretends not to care about the body,
but who really keeps on wishing for enjoyable things
is called a hypocrite.
Such a person is a fool.

यस्त्विन्द्रियाणि मनसा नियम्यारभतेऽर्जुन ।
कर्मेन्द्रियैः कर्मयोगमसक्तः स विशिष्यते ॥ ७ ॥
नियतं कुरु कर्म त्वं कर्म ज्यायो ह्यकर्मणः ।
शरीरयात्रापि च ते न प्रसिद्ध्येदकर्मणः ॥ ८ ॥
यज्ञार्थात्कर्मणोऽन्यत्र लोकोऽयं कर्मबन्धनः ।
तदर्थं कर्म कौन्तेय मुक्तसङ्गः समाचर ॥ ९ ॥
सहयज्ञाः प्रजाः सृष्ट्वा पुरोवाच प्रजापतिः ।
अनेन प्रसविष्यध्वमेष वोऽस्त्विष्टकामधुक् ॥ १० ॥
देवान्भावयतानेन ते देवा भावयन्तु वः ।
परस्परं भावयन्तः श्रेयः परमवाप्स्यथ ॥ ११ ॥
इष्टान्भोगान्हि वो देवा दास्यन्ते यज्ञभाविताः ।
तैर्दत्तानप्रदायैभ्यो यो भुङ्क्ते स्तेन एव सः ॥ १२ ॥
यज्ञशिष्टाशिनः सन्तो मुच्यन्ते सर्वकिल्बिषैः ।
भुञ्जते ते त्वघं पापा ये पचन्त्यात्मकारणात् ॥ १३ ॥
अन्नाद्भवन्ति भूतानि पर्जन्यादन्नसंभवः ।
यज्ञाद्भवति पर्जन्यो यज्ञः कर्मसमुद्भवः ॥ १४ ॥
कर्म ब्रह्मोद्भवं विद्धि ब्रह्माक्षरसमुद्भवम् ।
तस्मात्सर्वगतं ब्रह्म नित्यं यज्ञे प्रतिष्ठितम् ॥ १५ ॥

But a person who really and truly
does not care about her body is good.
She still takes care of her body
and uses it to do good things for God's sake
because she is good.
This is why I tell you action is best.
It is best to do your duty well.
Do it for God's sake and not for your own sake
and you will reach God.

People grow from food.
Food comes from rain.
Rain comes from prayers
and prayers are actions.
Actions come from the Vedas
and the Vedas come from God.
So action comes from God.

एवं प्रवर्तितं चक्रं नानुवर्तयतीह यः ।
अघायुरिन्द्रियारामो मोघं पार्थ स जीवति ॥१६॥
यस्त्वात्मरतिरेव स्यादात्मतृप्तश्च मानवः ।
आत्मन्येव च संतुष्टस्तस्य कार्यं न विद्यते ॥१७॥
नैव तस्य कृतेनार्थो नाकृतेनेह कश्चन ।
न चास्य सर्वभूतेषु कश्चिदर्थव्यपाश्रयः ॥१८॥
तस्मादसक्तः सततं कार्यं कर्म समाचर ।
असक्तो ह्याचरन्कर्म परमाप्नोति पूरुषः ॥१९॥
कर्मणैव हि संसिद्धिमास्थिता जनकादयः ।
लोकसङ्ग्रहमेवापि सम्पश्यन्कर्तुमर्हसि ॥२०॥
यद्यदाचरति श्रेष्ठस्तत्तदेवेतरो जनः ।
स यत्प्रमाणं कुरुते लोकस्तदनुवर्तते ॥२१॥

Arjun, life must follow this wheel
which turns and causes being born,
growing and dying.
Otherwise life has no meaning.

A man who cares only about himself
doesn't do his duty.
So always do your duty.
Do it as well as you can,
and don't worry
about how things will turn out.

Wise men as Janak
have become perfect in this way
and set an example
for other people to follow.

न मे पार्थास्ति कर्तव्यं त्रिषु लोकेषु किञ्चन ।
नानवाप्तमवाप्तव्यं वर्त एव च कर्मणि ॥२२॥
यदि ह्यहं न वर्तेयं जातु कर्मण्यतन्द्रितः ।
मम वर्त्मानुवर्तन्ते मनुष्याः पार्थ सर्वशः ॥२३॥
उत्सीदेयुरिमे लोका न कुर्यां कर्म चेदहम् ।
संकरस्य च कर्ता स्यामुपहन्यामिमाः प्रजाः ॥२४॥
सक्ताः कर्मण्यविद्वांसो यथा कुर्वन्ति भारत ।
कुर्याद्विद्वांस्तथाऽसक्तश्चिकीर्षुर्लोकसंग्रहम् ॥२५॥
न बुद्धिभेदं जनयेदज्ञानां कर्मसंगिनाम् ।
जोषयेत्सर्वकर्माणि विद्वान्युक्तः समाचरन् ॥२६॥
प्रकृतेः क्रियमाणानि गुणैः कर्माणि सर्वशः ।
अहंकारविमूढात्मा कर्ताहमिति मन्यते ॥२७॥
तत्त्ववित्तु महाबाहो गुणकर्मविभागयोः ।
गुणा गुणेषु वर्तन्त इति मत्वा न सज्जते ॥२८॥
प्रकृतेर्गुणसंमूढाः सज्जन्ते गुणकर्मसु ।
तानकृत्स्नविदो मन्दान्कृत्स्नविन्न विचालयेत् ॥२९॥
मयि सर्वाणि कर्माणि संन्यस्याध्यात्मचेतसा ।
निराशीर्निर्ममो भूत्वा युध्यस्व विगतज्वरः ॥३०॥

Oh Arjun,

there is nothing I, God, want but even I work.

If I stop working,

great trouble would come to the world,

for people would follow my example.

If I, God, give up actions,

if I stop doing good things,

the world would come to an end

and I would be the cause of confusion,

trouble and destruction.

Arjun, a fool does things for himself.

A wise woman does things for the world.

A wise woman knows

she does things only through God.

So go ahead. Do everything you should for My sake.

Do not wonder. Fight!

ये मे मतमिदं नित्यमनुतिष्ठन्ति मानवाः ।
श्रद्धावन्तोऽनसूयन्तो मुच्यन्ते तेऽपि कर्मभिः ॥३१॥
ये त्वेतदभ्यसूयन्तो नानुतिष्ठन्ति मे मतम् ।
सर्वज्ञानविमूढांस्तान्विद्धि नष्टानचेतसः ॥३२॥
सदृशं चेष्टते स्वस्याः प्रकृतेर्ज्ञानवानपि ।
प्रकृतिं यान्ति भूतानि निग्रहः किं करिष्यति ॥३३॥
इन्द्रियस्येन्द्रियस्यार्थे रागद्वेषौ व्यवस्थितौ ।
तयोर्न वशमागच्छेत्तौ ह्यस्य परिपन्थिनौ ॥३४॥
श्रेयान्स्वधर्मो विगुणः परधर्मात्स्वनुष्ठितात् ।
स्वधर्मे निधनं श्रेयः परधर्मो भयावहः ॥३५॥
अथ केन प्रयुक्तोऽयं पापं चरति पूरुषः ।
अनिच्छन्नपि वार्ष्णेय बलादिव नियोजितः ॥३६॥

Those who trust God
are on the road to Me.
Those who do not trust Me
are lost.

People need self control
to stop them from doing things
just because they feel like it.
People must do things which are their duty
whether they feel like doing them or not.
Your own duty is greater than anyone else's,
even if your duty is to die.

Then Arjun asked:
Why do some people sin?
Some people cannot help sinning.
They cannot help doing wrong things.

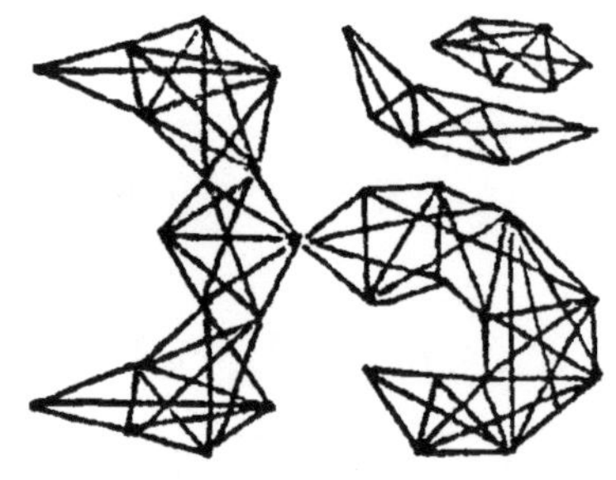

काम एष क्रोध एष रजोगुणसमुद्भवः ।
महाशनो महापाप्मा विद्ध्येनमिह वैरिणम् ॥३७॥
धूमेनाव्रियते वह्निर्यथाऽऽदर्शो मलेन च ।
यथोल्बेनावृतो गर्भस्तथा तेनेदमावृतम् ॥३८॥
आवृतं ज्ञानमेतेन ज्ञानिनो नित्यवैरिणा ।
कामरूपेण कौन्तेय दुष्पूरेणानलेन च ॥३९॥
इन्द्रियाणि मनो बुद्धिरस्याधिष्ठानमुच्यते ।
एतैर्विमोहयत्येष ज्ञानमावृत्य देहिनम् ॥४०॥
तस्मात्त्वमिन्द्रियाण्यादौ नियम्य भरतर्षभ ।
पाप्मानं प्रजहि ह्येनं ज्ञानविज्ञाननाशनम् ॥४१॥

Bhagvan answered:

Wanting things, desire makes people sin.
Wanting is bad.
It is greedy and evil and causes anger.
Getting what you want makes you greedy for more,
and not getting it makes you angry.
You must stop
forever wanting things for your body.

Desire covers the truth like dust covers a mirror
or like smoke covers fire.
Control yourself,
stop desire
and you will see the truth
and you will not sin.

Keep away from liking and hating,
two enemies who separate you from God.

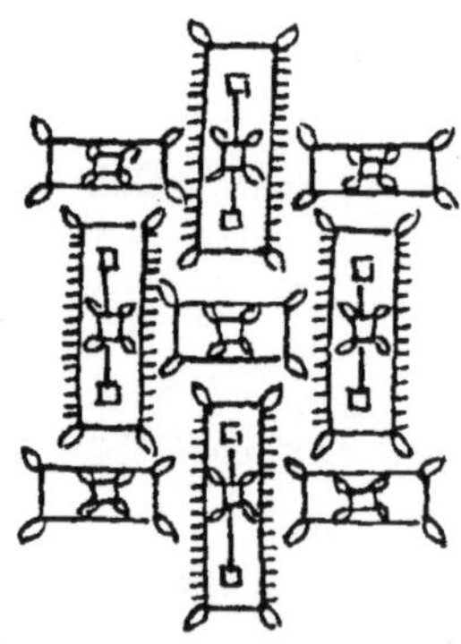

इन्द्रियाणि पराण्याहुरिन्द्रियेभ्यः परं मनः ।
मनसस्तु परा बुद्धिर्यो बुद्धेः परतस्तु सः ॥४२॥
एवं बुद्धेः परं बुद्ध्वा संस्तभ्यात्मानमात्मना ।
जहि शत्रुं महाबाहो कामरूपं दुरासदम् ॥४३॥

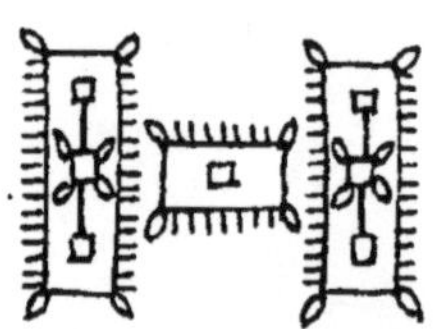

Remember, your mind is greater than your body.
And reason is even greater than your mind.
But your spirit, deep inside you,
is even greater than reason.

The mind controls the body
and tells it what to do.
Reason tells the mind
what is good and what is bad.
With reason you can control yourself.
With reason you can reach your spirit which is God.

Oh Arjun, control yourself.
Stop wanting one thing after another.
It is very hard to stop this,
but your reason will help you.
Control yourself and throw away sin.

श्री

चतुर्थोऽध्यायः

इमं विवस्वते योगं प्रोक्तवानहमव्ययम् ।
विवस्वान्मनवे प्राह मनुरिक्ष्वाकवेऽब्रवीत् ॥ १ ॥
एवं परंपराप्राप्तमिमं राजर्षयो विदुः ।
स कालेनेह महता योगो नष्टः परन्तप ॥ २ ॥
स एवायं मया तेऽद्य योगः प्रोक्तः पुरातनः ।
भक्तोऽसि मे सखा चेति रहस्यं ह्येतदुत्तमम् ॥ ३ ॥
अपरं भवतो जन्म परं जन्म विवस्वतः ।
कथमेतद्विजानीयां त्वमादौ प्रोक्तवानिति ॥ ४ ॥

Chapter 4

The Sword of Knowledge

Bhagvan said:
I have taught the truth to Vivaswan,
the Sun God;
Vivaswan taught it to his son Manu
and Manu taught it to his son Ishvaku.
And today I teach it to you,
because you love Me and are My friend.
This truth is very secret.

Arjun replied:
But Visvaswan lived long ago.
Did you teach
at the beginning of the world?

बहूनि मे व्यतीतानि जन्मानि तव चार्जुन ।
तान्यहं वेद सर्वाणि न त्वं वेत्थ परन्तप ॥ ५ ॥
अजोऽपि सन्नव्ययात्मा भूतानामीश्वरोऽपि सन् ।
प्रकृतिं स्वामधिष्ठाय संभवाम्यात्ममायया ॥ ६ ॥
यदा यदा हि धर्मस्य ग्लानिर्भवति भारत ।
अभ्युत्थानमधर्मस्य तदाऽऽत्मानं सृजाम्यहम् ॥ ७ ॥
परित्राणाय साधूनां विनाशाय च दुष्कृताम् ।
धर्मसंस्थापनार्थाय संभवामि युगे युगे ॥ ८ ॥
जन्म कर्म च मे दिव्यमेवं यो वेत्ति तत्त्वतः ।
त्यक्त्वा देहं पुनर्जन्म नैति मामेति सोऽर्जुन ॥ ९ ॥
वीतरागभयक्रोधा मन्मया मामुपाश्रिताः ।
बहवो ज्ञानतपसा पूता मद्भावमागताः ॥ १० ॥
ये यथा मां प्रपद्यन्ते तांस्तथैव भजाम्यहम् ।
मम वर्त्मानुवर्तन्ते मनुष्याः पार्थ सर्वशः ॥ ११ ॥
काङ्क्षन्तः कर्मणां सिद्धिं यजन्त इह देवताः ।
क्षिप्रं हि मानुषे लोके सिद्धिर्भवति कर्मजा ॥ १२ ॥

Bhagvan answered:

You and I have passed through many births.

I know them all but you do not remember.

I am born from time to time

whenever the good need my protection.

I am born to destroy the bad and help the good.

My birth is divine and those who understand this

become part of Me

and do not have to be born again.

Many people have become pure.

They have become wise

and they have concentrated on Me.

They have become part of Me.

People look for Me and I too look for them.

चातुर्वर्ण्यं मया सृष्टं गणकर्मविभागशः ।
तस्य कर्तारमपि मां विद्धयकर्तारमव्ययम् ॥१३॥
न मां कर्माणि लिम्पन्ति न मे कर्मफले स्पृहा ।
इति मां योऽभिजानाति कर्मभिर्न स बुद्धयते ॥१४॥

एवं ज्ञात्वा कृतं कर्म पूर्वैरपि मुमुक्षुभिः ।
कुरु कर्मैव तस्मात्त्वं पूर्वैः पूर्वतरं कृतम् ॥१५॥
किं कर्म किमकर्मेति कवयोऽप्यत्र मोहिताः ।
तत्ते कर्म प्रवक्ष्यामि यज्ज्ञात्वा मोक्ष्यसेऽशुभात् ॥१६॥

I made the four groups of people for the world
and divided people
according to their natures and work.
These groups are priests, warriors,
business people and servants.

From very early times,
people who wanted to reach Me
and become part of Me
did not stop doing everyday things
while they concentrated on Me.
But even wise men
do not understand how to do this.
So I will explain the truth to you.
I will tell you
how you can be free from action
without stopping it.

33

कर्मणो ह्यपि बोद्धव्यं बोद्धव्यं च विकर्मणः ।
अकर्मणश्च बोद्धव्यं गहना कर्मणो गतिः ॥१७॥
कर्मण्यकर्म यः पश्येदकर्मणि च कर्म यः ।
स बुद्धिमान्मनुष्येषु स युक्तः कृत्स्नकर्मकृत् ॥१८॥

If you become free from action,
you do not have to be born
again and again.
You will not need a new life
to finish what you started in your old life.
You will not be tied
to the circle of birth and death.
But you do not have to stop doing things
to be freed
from the things you do.
You can act and still be free.

I will explain good action, doing good things;
bad action, doing things which are not allowed;
and inaction, doing nothing.
All this is a real mystery.
All this is hard to understand.

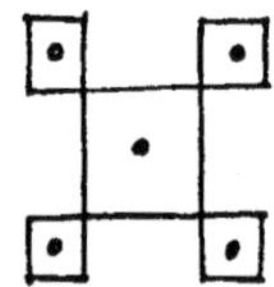

यस्य सर्वे समारम्भाः कामसंकल्पवर्जिताः ।
ज्ञानाग्निदग्धकर्माणं तमाहुः पण्डितं बुधाः ॥१९॥

त्यक्त्वा कर्मफलासङ्गं नित्यतृप्तो निराश्रयः ।
कर्मण्यभिप्रवृत्तोऽपि नैव किञ्चित्करोति सः ॥२०॥

निराशीर्यतचित्तात्मा त्यक्तसर्वपरिग्रहः ।
शारीरं केवलं कर्म कुर्वन्नाप्नोति किल्बिषम् ॥२१॥

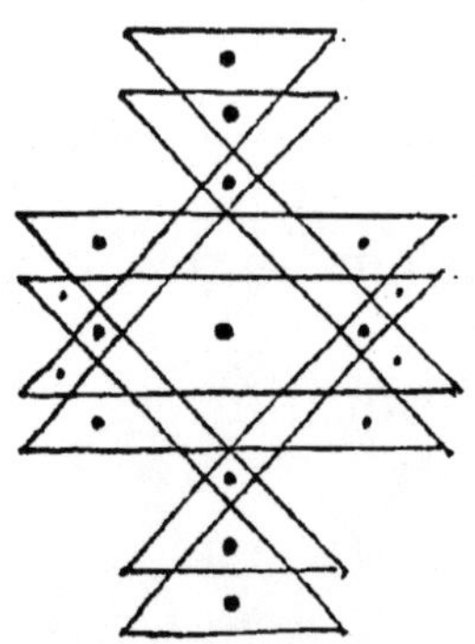

It is hard to understand that the wise are free
because they do nothing while they do their duty.
The secret is doing your duty for God's sake.

A person who does everything just for God's sake
is wise.
She is always happy.
She does not want or need anything
and so she is free.
She is calm while she does her duty.
Her mind is doing nothing except
concentrating on God.

A person who is wise never sins.
She is always cheerful.
She is not jealous.
She is past happiness and unhappiness.

यदृच्छालाभसंतुष्टो द्वन्द्वातीतो विमत्सरः ।
समः सिद्धावसिद्धौ च कृत्वापि न निबध्यते ॥२२॥

गतसङ्गस्य मुक्तस्य ज्ञानावस्थितचेतसः ।
यज्ञायाचरतः कर्म समग्रं प्रविलीयते ॥२३॥

ब्रह्मार्पणं ब्रह्म हविर्ब्रह्माग्नौ ब्रह्मणा हुतम् ।
ब्रह्मैव तेन गन्तव्यं ब्रह्मकर्मसमाधिना ॥२४॥

The wise person is free.
He does not have to be born again.
The things he does
do not give him any punishments or rewards,
so he does not need another life
in which to be punished or rewarded.

A person who does everything for God's sake
is free and becomes a part of God.
Doing your duty only for God's sake
is the secret.

A puja is a ceremony for God.
It is a sacrifice.
The puja is Brahma.
The fire which is part of the puja is Brahma.
The person who performs the puja is Brahma.

दैवमेवापरे यज्ञं योगिनः पर्युपासते ।
ब्रह्माग्नावपरे यज्ञं यज्ञेनैवोपजुह्वति ॥२५॥
श्रोत्रादीनीन्द्रियाण्यन्ये संयमाग्निषु जह्वति ।
शब्दादीन्विषयानन्य इन्द्रियाग्निषु जह्वति ॥२६॥
सर्वाणीन्द्रियकर्माणि प्राणकर्माणि चापरे ।
आत्मसंयमयोगाग्नौ जुह्वति ज्ञानदीपिते ॥२७॥
द्रव्ययज्ञास्तपोयज्ञा योगयज्ञास्तथाऽपरे ।
स्वाध्यायज्ञानयज्ञाश्च यतयः संशितव्रताः ॥२८॥
अपाने जुह्वति प्राणं प्राणेऽपानं तथाऽपरे ।
प्राणापानगती रुद्ध्वा प्राणायामपरायणाः ॥२९॥
अपरे नियताहाराः प्राणान्प्राणेषु जुह्वति ।
सर्वेऽप्येते यज्ञविदो यज्ञक्षपितकल्मषाः ॥३०॥
यज्ञशिष्टामृतभुजो यान्ति ब्रह्म सनातनम् ।
नायं लोकोऽस्त्ययज्ञस्य कुतोऽन्यः कुरुसत्तम ॥३१॥
एवं बहुविधा यज्ञा वितता ब्रह्मणो मुखे ।
कर्मजान्विद्धि तान्सर्वानेवं ज्ञात्वा विमोक्ष्यसे ॥३२॥
श्रेयान्द्रव्यमयाद्यज्ञाज्ज्ञानयज्ञः परन्तप ।
सर्वं कर्माखिलं पार्थ ज्ञाने परिसमाप्यते ॥३३॥

ॐ

Brahma is God's absolute, everlasting power.
We cannot see or hear or feel Brahma.
Reaching Brahma and understanding Brahma
is the reason for the puja.

A sacrifice is giving something up for God.
It is doing something for God's sake.
Some people give things up for God.
Some people suffer for God's sake.
Some study for God's sake.
Some breathe for God's sake.
All these people sacrifice for God
and their sins are washed away.

But sacrifice that is knowledge
is better than giving up things.
Learning the truth for God's sake
is the best sacrifice.

तद्विद्धि प्रणिपातेन परिप्रश्नेन सेवया ।
उपदेक्ष्यन्ति ते ज्ञानं ज्ञानिनस्तत्त्वदर्शिनः ॥३४॥

यज्ज्ञात्वा न पुनर्मोहमेवं यास्यसि पाण्डव ।
येन भूतान्यशेषेण द्रक्ष्यस्यात्मन्यथो मयि ॥३५॥

अपि चेदसि पापेभ्यः सर्वेभ्यः पापकृत्तमः ।
सर्वं ज्ञानप्लवेनैव वृजिनं सन्तरिष्यसि ॥३६॥

To get knowledge means to learn the truth.
To learn you must bow down with respect to the wise.
You must serve them and wait on them
with a pure heart
and they will teach the truth to you.

Then, Arjun, when you know the truth,
you will not doubt any more.
You will not be mixed up.
You will see the whole world
in your own heart
and then in God.

Even the worst sinner can become good
and reach God through knowledge.
Knowledge is like a boat which takes you
across the ocean of sin.

यथैधांसि समिद्धोऽग्निर्भस्मसात्कुरुतेऽर्जुन ।
ज्ञानाग्निः सर्वकर्माणि भस्मसात्कुरुते तथा ॥३७॥
नहि ज्ञानेन सदृशं पवित्रमिह विद्यते ।
तत्स्वयं योगसंसिद्धः कालेनात्मनि विन्दति ॥३८॥

श्रद्धावाँल्लभते ज्ञानं तत्परः संयतेन्द्रियः ।
ज्ञानं लब्ध्वा परां शांतिमचिरेणाधिगच्छति ॥३९॥
अज्ञश्चाश्रद्दधानश्च संशयात्मा विनश्यति ।
नायं लोकोऽस्ति न परो न सुखं संशयात्मनः ॥४०॥

योगसंन्यस्तकर्माणं ज्ञानसंछिन्नसंशयम् ।
आत्मवन्तं न कर्माणि निबध्नन्ति धनञ्जय ॥४१॥
तस्मादज्ञानसंभूतं हृत्स्थं ज्ञानासिनात्मनः ।
छित्त्वैनं संशयं योगमातिष्ठोत्तिष्ठ भारत ॥४२॥

Like a fire burns wood to ashes,
the fire of knowledge burns the things you do to ashes
and these burnt actions
give you no punishments and no rewards.
This is how knowing the truth makes you free.

Knowing the truth takes you right to God.

If you have no faith, no trust in God,
you will doubt and lose God and be unhappy.

Oh Arjun, do everything for God's sake.
The doubt in your heart
is the doubt of not knowing the truth.
With the sword of knowledge, cut this doubt out.
Be free.
Do your duty for God's sake.
Stand up and fight!

श्री

पञ्चमोऽध्यायः

संन्यासं कर्मणां कृष्ण पुनर्योगं च शंससि ।
यच्छ्रेय एतयोरेकं तन्मे ब्रूहि सुनिश्चितम् ॥ १ ॥

संन्यासः कर्मयोगश्च निःश्रेयसकरावुभौ ।
तयोस्तु कर्मसंन्यासात्कर्मयोगो विशिष्यते ॥ २ ॥

Chapter 5

The Two Paths

Arjun said:

Lord Krishna,

You praise knowing the truth

and then You praise doing good.

Please tell me clearly

which of the two is best.

Bhagvan answered:

Knowledge is knowing truth;

action is doing good.

Both are excellent paths to God.

But doing good is easier

and so it is best.

ज्ञेयः स नित्यसंन्यासी यो न द्वेष्टि न कांक्षति ।
निर्द्वन्द्वो हि महाबाहो सुखं बन्धात्प्रमुच्यते ॥ ३ ॥

सांख्ययोगौ पृथग्बालाः प्रवदन्ति न पण्डिताः ।
एकमप्यास्थितः सम्यगुभयोर्विन्दते फलम् ॥ ४ ॥

यत्सांख्यैः प्राप्यते स्थानं तद्योगैरपि गम्यते ।
एकं सांख्यं च योगं च यः पश्यति स पश्यति ॥ ५ ॥

The man who does good,
the man who does his duty for God's sake alone
is called a Karmayogi.
Such a man is also a Sanyasi,
which means a person who has given up
everything for God.
This man is beyond the world and is part of God.

Only fools think the paths
of knowledge and learning are separate.
Because a person reaches God by either path.
The wise man understands
that both paths are really one.

He who sees that action and knowledge are the same
sees truth.

संन्यासस्तु महाबाहो दुःखमाप्तुमयोगतः ।
योगयुक्तो मुनिर्ब्रह्म न चिरेणाधिगच्छति ॥ ६ ॥
योगयुक्तो विशुद्धात्मा विजितात्मा जितेन्द्रियः ।
सर्वभूतात्मभूतात्मा कुर्वन्नपि न लिप्यते ॥ ७ ॥
नैव किंचित्करोमीति युक्तो मन्येत तत्त्ववित् ।
पश्यन्शृण्वन्स्पृशञ्जिघ्रन्नश्नन्गच्छन्स्वपन्श्वसन् ॥ ८ ॥
प्रलपन्विसृजन्गृह्णन्नुन्मिषन्निमिषन्नपि ।
इन्द्रियाणीन्द्रियार्थेषु वर्तन्त इति धारयन् ॥ ९ ॥
ब्रह्मण्याधाय कर्माणि सङ्गं त्यक्त्वा करोति यः ।
लिप्यते न स पापेन पद्मपत्रमिवाम्भसा ॥१०॥
कायेन मनसा बुद्ध्या केवलैरिन्द्रियैरपि ।
योगिनः कर्म कुर्वन्ति सङ्गं त्यक्त्वात्मशुद्धये ॥११॥
युक्तः कर्मफलं त्यक्त्वा शान्तिमाप्नोति नैष्ठिकीम् ।
अयुक्तः कामकारेण फले सक्तो निबध्यते ॥१२॥
सर्वकर्माणि मनसा संन्यस्यास्ते सुखं वशी ।
नवद्वारे पुरे देही नैव कुर्वन्न कारयन् ॥१३॥
न कर्तृत्वं न कर्माणि लोकस्य सृजति प्रभुः ।
न कर्मफलसंयोगं स्वभावस्तु प्रवर्तते ॥१४॥
नादत्ते कस्यचित्पापं न चैव सुकृतं विभुः ।
अज्ञानेनावृतं ज्ञानं तेन मुह्यन्ति जन्तवः ॥१५॥

The Karmayogi does everything for God.
His mind is on God while he acts.
He wakes, sleeps, hears, sees, touches,
smells, speaks and breathes thinking of God.
He understands that he himself does nothing
but that God does everything through him.
God uses him to get things done.
The person who offers all he does to God
is as untouched by sin as a lotus leaf by water.
The Karmayogi is pure.

The person who does everything only for God
is peaceful and becomes part of God.
The Karmayogi is past all this.
God does not share the punishments
or rewards of people.

ज्ञानेन तु तदज्ञानं येषां नाशितमात्मनः ।
तेषामादित्यवज्ज्ञानं प्रकाशयति तत्परम् ॥१६॥
तद्बुद्धयस्तदात्मानस्तन्निष्ठास्तत्परायणाः ।
गच्छन्त्यपुनरावृत्तिं ज्ञाननिर्धूतकल्मषाः ॥१७॥

विद्याविनयसंपन्ने ब्राह्मणे गवि हस्तिनि ।
शुनि चैव श्वपाके च पण्डिताः समदर्शिनः ॥१८॥
इहैव तैर्जितः सर्गो येषां साम्ये स्थितं मनः ।
निर्दोषं हि समं ब्रह्म तस्माद्ब्रह्मणि ते स्थिताः ॥१९॥

न प्रहृष्येत्प्रियं प्राप्य नोद्विजेत्प्राप्य चाप्रियम् ।
स्थिरबुद्धिरसंमूढो ब्रह्मविद्ब्रह्मणि स्थितः ॥२०॥
बाह्यस्पर्शेष्वसक्तात्मा विन्दत्यात्मनि यत्सुखम् ।
स ब्रह्मयोगयुक्तात्मा सुखमक्षयमश्नुते ॥२१॥

God shines like the sun on the wise.
The wise are mixed in God.
They are part of God.
They adore Him
and their sins are washed away.

The wise give the same love
to a Brahmin, a cow,
an elephant or a dog.
They understand God is in all.
The wise live forever.

The wise person considers happiness
and unhappiness the same.
He is always happy
because he is with God.
His mind is strong
because it is with God.

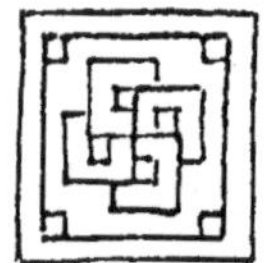

ये हि संस्पर्शजा भोगा दुःखयोनय एव ते ।
आद्यन्तवन्तः कौन्तेय न तेषु रमते बुधः ॥२२॥

शक्नोतीहैव यः सोढुं प्राक् शरीरविमोक्षणात् ।
कामक्रोधोद्भवं वेगं स युक्तः स सुखी नरः ॥२३॥

योऽन्तःसुखोऽन्तरारामस्तथान्तर्ज्योतिरेव यः ।
स योगी ब्रह्मनिर्वाणं ब्रह्मभूतोऽधिगच्छति ॥२४॥

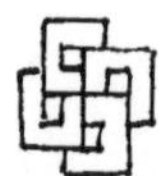

Pleasures that come from the body
are really pains
because they come to an end.
That is why a wise man does not care about them.

The wise person can stand here on earth
and not care about his body
which makes him want things
and then get angry.

The happy person is wise.
His soul shines brightly.
The happy person is peaceful.
He reaches God and God is peace.

The happiness and joy of the wise man
come from inside himself.

लभन्ते ब्रह्मनिर्वाणमृषयः क्षीणकल्मषाः ।
छिन्नद्वैधा यतात्मानः सर्वभूतहिते रताः ॥२५॥

कामक्रोधवियुक्तानां यतीनां यतचेतसाम् ।
अभितो ब्रह्मनिर्वाणं वर्तते विदितात्मनाम् ॥२६॥

स्पर्शान्कृत्वा बहिर्बाह्यांश्चक्षुश्चैवान्तरे भ्रुवोः ।
प्राणापानौ समौ कृत्वा नासाभ्यन्तरचारिणौ ॥२७॥

यतेन्द्रियमनोबुद्धिर्मुनिर्मोक्षपरायणः ।
विगतेच्छाभयक्रोधो यः सदा मुक्त एव सः ॥२८॥

भोक्तारं यज्ञतपसां सर्वलोकमहेश्वरम् ।
सुहृदं सर्वभूतानां ज्ञात्वा मां शान्तिमृच्छति ॥२९॥

Wise happy persons shut everything out of their mind
except God.
Their eyes look straight ahead.
Their breathing is steady.
Their mind is calm
and concentrates on God.
Such persons want nothing.
They are not angry.
They are not afraid.
They are free.

Those who truly love Me know
I am God of the whole world.
They know I am the friend of all.
They who really love Me
know everlasting peacefulness
and everlasting happiness.

श्री

षष्ठोऽध्यायः

अनाश्रितः कर्मफलं कार्यं कर्म करोति यः ।
स संन्यासी च योगी च न निरग्निर्न चाक्रियः ॥ १ ॥
यं सन्यासमिति प्राहुर्योगं तं विद्धि पाण्डव ।
न ह्यसंन्यस्तसंकल्पो योगी भवति कश्चन ॥ २ ॥

ॐ

आरुरुक्षोर्मुनेर्योगं कर्म कारणमुच्यते ।
योगारूढस्य तस्यैव शमः कारणमुच्यते ॥ ३ ॥
यदा हि नेन्द्रियार्थेषु न कर्मस्वनुषज्जते ।
सर्वसंकल्पसंन्यासी योगारूढस्तदोच्यते ॥ ४ ॥

उद्धरेदात्मनात्मानं नात्मानमवसादयेत् ।
आत्मैव ह्यात्मनो बन्धुरात्मैव रिपुरात्मनः ॥ ५ ॥
बन्धुरात्मात्मनस्तस्य येनात्मैवात्मना जितः ।
अनात्मनस्तु शत्रुत्वे वर्तेतात्मैव शत्रुवत् ॥ ६ ॥

Chapter 6

Self Control

Bhagvan said:

Doing things for no reward,
doing them for God's sake
is like climbing a ladder to God.

You should lift yourself to God
by your own work.
You should not lower yourself.
You are your own friend and your own enemy.

You are your own friend if your spirit rules your body.
You are your own enemy if your body rules your spirit.
Your spirit is part of God.

जितात्मनः प्रशान्तस्य परमात्मा समाहितः ।
शीतोष्णसुखदुःखेषु तथा मानापमानयोः ॥ ७ ॥

ज्ञानविज्ञानतृप्तात्मा कूटस्थो विजितेन्द्रियः ।
युक्त इत्युच्यते योगी समलोष्टाश्मकाञ्चनः ॥ ८ ॥

सुहृन्मित्रार्युदासीनमध्यस्थद्वेष्यबन्धुषु ।
साधुष्वपि च पापेषु समबुद्धिर्विशिष्यते ॥ ९ ॥

Because of this,

the person whose spirit rules her completely

is ruled by God.

This person has self control.

She is calm, no matter what happens.

She is calm if she is cold or hot.

She is calm if she is comfortable or uncomfortable.

She is calm if she is praised or criticized.

The person who has self control never changes.

A piece of stone and gold are the same to her.

A wise person like this is called a Yogi.

The Yogi likes friends as much as enemies;

he likes his family as well as strangers.

योगी युञ्जीत सततमात्मानं रहसि स्थितः ।
एकाकी यतचित्तात्मा निराशीरपरिग्रहः ॥१०॥
शुचौ देशे प्रतिष्ठाप्य स्थिरमासनमात्मनः ।
नात्युच्छ्रितं नातिनीचं चैलाजिनकुशोत्तरम् ॥११॥
तत्रैकाग्रं मनः कृत्वा यतचित्तेन्द्रियक्रियः ।
उपविश्यासने युञ्ज्याद्योगमात्मविशुद्धये ॥१२॥
समं कायशिरोग्रीवं धारयन्नचलं स्थिरः ।
संप्रेक्ष्य नासिकाग्रं स्वं दिशश्चानवलोकयन् ॥१३॥

ॐ

प्रशान्तात्मा विगतभीर्ब्रह्मचारिव्रते स्थितः ।
मनः संयम्य मच्चित्तो युक्त आसीत मत्परः ॥१४॥

युञ्जन्नेवं सदात्मानं योगी नियतमानसः ।
शान्तिं निर्वाणपरमां मत्संस्थामधिगच्छति ॥१५॥
नात्यश्नतस्तु योगोऽस्ति न चैकान्तमनश्नतः ।
न चातिस्वप्नशीलस्य जाग्रतो नैव चार्जुन ॥१६॥
युक्ताहारविहारस्य युक्तचेष्टस्य कर्मसु ।
युक्तस्वप्नावबोधस्य योगो भवति दुःखहा ॥१७॥
यदा विनियतं चित्तमात्मन्येवावतिष्ठते ।
निःस्पृहः सर्वकामेभ्यो युक्त इत्युच्यते तदा ॥१८॥

A Yogi who is alone
should find a clean place on the grass
and spread a cloth to sit upon.
Here he should sit and control his mind.
He should sit up straight
and look steadily at the tip of his nose,
not moving at all.
In this position,
a Yogi must think only of God
until he finds everlasting happiness.
Thinking peacefully of God is called meditation.

Oh Arjun, a Yogi cannot eat too much or too little.
She cannot sleep too much or too little.
She must measure everything:
eating, sleeping, working and relaxing.
Everything she does
should be just right and even.

यथा दीपो निवातस्थो नेङ्गते सोपमा स्मृता ।
योगिनो यतचित्तस्य युञ्जतो योगमात्मनः ॥१९॥
यत्रोपरमते चित्तं निरुद्धं योगसेवया ।
यत्र चैवात्मनात्मानं पश्यन्नात्मनि तुष्यति ॥२०॥
सुखमात्यन्तिकं यत्तद्बुद्धिग्राह्यमतीन्द्रियम् ।
वेत्ति यत्र न चैवायं स्थितश्चलति तत्त्वतः ॥२१॥
यं लब्ध्वा चापरं लाभं मन्यते नाधिकं ततः ।
यस्मिन्स्थितो न दुःखेन गुरुणापि विचाल्यते ॥२२॥
तं विद्याद्दुःखसंयोगवियोगं योगसंज्ञितम् ।
स निश्चयेन योक्तव्यो योगोऽनिर्विण्णचेतसा ॥२३॥

संकल्पप्रभवान्कामांस्त्यक्त्वा सर्वानशेषतः ।
मनसैवेन्द्रियग्रामं विनियम्य समन्ततः ॥२४॥
शनैः शनैरुपरमेद्बुद्ध्या धृतिगृहीतया ।
आत्मसंस्थं मनः कृत्वा न किञ्चिदपि चिन्तयेत् ॥२५॥
यतो यतो निश्चरति मनश्चञ्चलमस्थिरम् ।
ततस्ततो नियम्यैतदात्मन्येव वशं नयेत् ॥२६॥
प्रशान्तमनसं ह्येनं योगिनं सुखमुत्तमम् ।
उपैति शान्तरजसं ब्रह्मभूतमकल्मषम् ॥२७॥
युञ्जन्नेवं सदात्मानं योगी विगतकल्मषः ।
सुखेन ब्रह्मसंस्पर्शमत्यन्तं सुखमश्नुते ॥२८॥

A Yogi is never afraid.

The Yogi whose mind is concentrating on God
does not shake.
He is steady
like a candle in a room where there is no wind.
The Yogi's mind does not move away from the truth.

To become a Yogi
you have to practice being calm.
You have to practice not fidgeting
and concentrating on God.

And the Yogi who is perfectly calm
is pure and free of sin.
He is one with God
and perfectly happy.

सर्वभूतस्थमात्मानं सर्वभूतानि चात्मनि ।
ईक्षते योगयुक्तात्मा सर्वत्र समदर्शनः ॥२९॥
यो मां पश्यति सर्वत्र सर्वं च मयि पश्यति ।
तस्याहं न प्रणश्यामि स च मे न प्रणश्यति ॥३०॥
सर्वभूतस्थितं यो मां भजत्येकत्वमास्थितः ।
सर्वथा वर्तमानोऽपि स योगी मयि वर्तते ॥३१॥
आत्मौपम्येन सर्वत्र समं पश्यति योऽर्जुन ।
सुखं वा यदि वा दुःखं स योगी परमो मतः ॥३२॥

योऽयं योगस्त्वया प्रोक्तः साम्येन मधुसूदन ।
एतस्याहं न पश्यामि चञ्चलत्वात्स्थितिं स्थिराम् ॥३३॥
चञ्चलं हि मनः कृष्ण प्रमाथि बलवद्दृढम् ।
तस्याहं निग्रहं मन्ये वायोरिव सुदुष्करम् ॥३४॥
असंशयं महाबाहो मनो दुर्निग्रहं चलम् ।
अभ्यासेन तु कौन्तेय वैराग्येण च गृह्यते ॥३५॥
असंयतात्मना योगो दुष्प्राप इति मे मतिः ।
वश्यात्मना तु यतता शक्योऽवाप्तुमुपायतः ॥३६॥

He understands that everything in the world is One.
He sees everything in Me, God and God in everything.

The Yogi who realizes God is everywhere
never loses Me
and I never lose him.

Arjun said:
But it is hard to control the mind.
The mind is strong and jumpy
and as hard to control as the wind.

Bhagvan answered:
I know it is hard to control the mind.
But you can control your mind
little by little
if you practice steadily.

अयतिः श्रद्धयोपेतो योगाच्चलितमानसः ।
अप्राप्य योगसंसिद्धिं कां गतिं कृष्ण गच्छति ॥३७॥
कच्चिन्नोभयविभ्रष्टश्छिन्नाभ्रमिव नश्यति ।
अप्रतिष्ठो महाबाहो विमूढो ब्रह्मणः पथि ॥३८॥
एतन्मे संशयं कृष्ण छेत्तुमर्हस्यशेषतः ।
त्वदन्यः संशयस्यास्य छेत्ता न ह्युपपद्यते ॥३९॥
पार्थ नैवेह नामुत्र विनाशस्तस्य विद्यते ।
नहि कल्याणकृत्कश्चिद्‌दुर्गतिं तात गच्छति ॥४०॥

प्राप्य पुण्यकृताँल्लोकानुषित्वा शाश्वतीः समाः ।
शुचीनां श्रीमतां गेहे योगभ्रष्टोऽभिजायते ॥४१॥
अथवा योगिनामेव कुले भवति धीमताम् ।
एतद्धि दुर्लभतरं लोके जन्म यदीदृशम् ॥४२॥
तत्र तं बुद्धिसंयोगं लभते पौर्वदेहिकम् ।
यतते च ततो भूयः संसिद्धौ कुरुनन्दन ॥४३॥
पूर्वाभ्यासेन तेनैव ह्रियते ह्यवशोऽपि सः ।
जिज्ञासुरपि योगस्य शब्दब्रह्मातिवर्तते ॥४४॥

Arjun asked again:

What happens to people who love God

but have not learned to control their mind

even though they tried?

And Bhagvan answered:

Nothing bad happens to such people if they have tried.

Only good can happen to people

who have really tried to reach God.

They will go to heaven

and after spending countless years there,

they will be born again in a good family.

Then they will try again to reach God.

They will start where they stopped in their earlier life.

They will not have to begin all over because

their spirit will remember what they learned before.

They will feel pulled to God.

प्रयत्नाद्यतमानस्तु योगी संशुद्धकिल्बिषः ।
अनेकजन्मसंसिद्धस्ततो याति परां गतिम् ॥४५॥

तपस्विभ्योऽधिको योगी ज्ञानिभ्योऽपि मतोऽधिकः ।
कर्मिभ्यश्चाधिको योगी तस्माद्योगी भवार्जुन ॥४६॥

योगिनामपि सर्वेषां मद्गतेनान्तरात्मना ।
श्रद्धावान्भजते यो मां स मे युक्ततमो मतः ॥४७॥

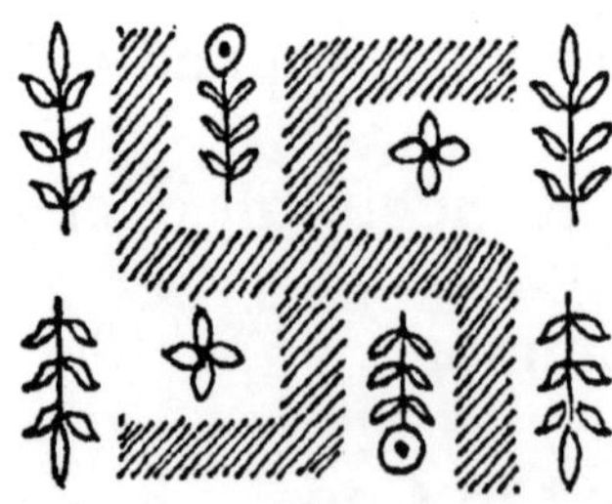

But the Yogi who controls his mind
is perfect.
He is forever happy.

For this reason,
Oh Arjun,
be a Yogi.
Learn self control
and love Me
with all your heart.

श्री

सप्तमोऽध्यायः

मय्यासक्तमनाः पार्थ योगं युञ्जन्मदाश्रयः ।
असंशयं समग्रं मां यथा ज्ञास्यसि तच्छृणु ॥ १ ॥

ज्ञानं तेऽहं सविज्ञानमिदं वक्ष्याम्यशेषतः ।
यज्ज्ञात्वा नेह भूयोऽन्यज्ज्ञातव्यमवशिष्यते ॥ २ ॥

मनुष्याणां सहस्रेषु कश्चिद्यतति सिद्धये ।
यततामपि सिद्धानां कश्चिन्मां वेत्ति तत्त्वतः ॥ ३ ॥

Chapter 7

Knowing God

Bhagvan said:

Arjun, listen now
to how by thinking of Me and loving Me
you will know Me and be sure about Me.
I will help you to understand
and after you know God,
nothing in the world will be a secret.

Of thousands and thousands of people,
only a few try to know Me.
And of the few who try,
just a handful of special ones
really understand God completely.

भूमिरापोऽनलो वायुः खं मनो बुद्धिरेव च ।
अहंकार इतीयं मे भिन्ना प्रकृतिरष्टधा ॥४॥

अपरेयमितस्त्वन्यां प्रकृतिं विद्धि मे पराम् ।
जीवभूतां महाबाहो ययेदं धार्यते जगत् ॥५॥

एतद्योनीनि भूतानि सर्वाणीत्युपधारय ।
अहं कृत्स्नस्य जगतः प्रभवः प्रलयस्तथा ॥६॥

मत्तः परतरं नान्यत्किञ्चिदस्ति धनञ्जय ।
मयि सर्वमिदं प्रोतं सूत्रे मणिगणा इव ॥७॥

रसोऽहमप्सु कौन्तेय प्रभाऽस्मि शशिसूर्ययोः ।
प्रणवः सर्ववेदेषु शब्दः खे पौरुषं नृषु ॥८॥

I am made of earth, water, fire, air,
ether, mind, reason, and the self.
These eight things are one side of Me.
The other, higher, side of Me
is what makes the whole world exist
and is called the "life principle."

Arjun, now you know that everything comes from Me
and it all will turn back into Me.
And there is nothing in the world but Me.
And I am God.

I am the wetness in water,
the light in the moon and the sun;
I am Om in the Vedas.
"Om" is God's magic word.

पुण्यो गन्धः पृथिव्यां च तेजश्चास्मि विभावसौ ।
जीवनं सर्वभूतेषु तपश्चास्मि तपस्विषु ॥ ९ ॥

बीजं मां सर्वभूतानां विद्धि पार्थ सनातनम् ।
बुद्धिर्बुद्धिमतामस्मि तेजस्तेजस्विनामहम् ॥१०॥

बलं बलवतां चाहं कामरागविवर्जितम् ।
धर्माविरुद्धो भूतेषु कामोऽस्मि भरतर्षभ ॥११॥

ये चैव सात्त्विका भावा राजसास्तामसाश्च ये ।
मत्त एवेति तान्विद्धि न त्वहं तेषु ते मयि ॥१२॥

त्रिभिर्गुणमयैर्भावैरेभिः सर्वमिदं जगत् ।
मोहितं नाभिजानाति मामेभ्यः परमव्ययम् ॥१३॥

I am the manliness in men
and the smell of the earth
and the brightness in fire.
I am life in living things.

I am the seed in all beings.
I am the wisdom in men's minds.
I am the strength of the strong
and the wish in your heart.

Everyone thinks that the things in the world are real,
but only I, God, am real and unchanging.
Everything else is make believe.
Only people who understand God can understand this.
Only the wise can understand
that God alone is real.

55

दैवी ह्येषा गुणमयी मम माया दुरत्यया ।
मामेव ये प्रपद्यन्ते मायामेतां तरन्ति ते ॥१४॥

न मां दुष्कृतिनो मूढाः प्रपद्यन्ते नराधमाः ।
माययापहृतज्ञाना आसुरं भावमाश्रिताः ॥१५॥

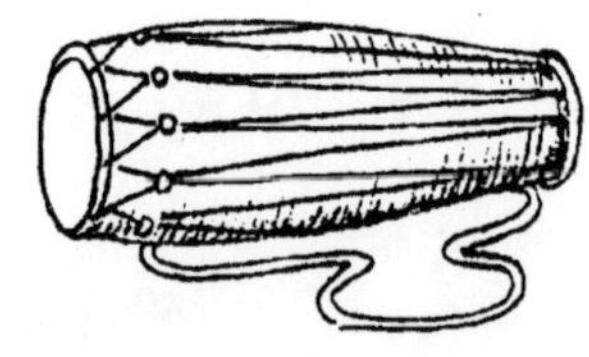

The world seems real because I use My divine Maya
to make it appear.
"Maya" is make-believe. It is magic.
It causes the world and everything in it
to seem solid and permanent.

But the things in the world are always moving
and always changing.
That is why they are not real
and they do not last forever.
Only God is forever real.

The wise who understand God pass beyond the world.
They cross over Maya and reach Me.

Fools and evil people do not understand Me.
They do not worship Me.

चतुर्विधा भजन्ते मां जनाः सुकृतिनोऽर्जुन ।
आर्तो जिज्ञासुरर्थार्थी ज्ञानी च भरतर्षभ ॥१६॥
तेषां ज्ञानी नित्ययुक्त एकभक्तिर्विशिष्यते ।
प्रियो हि ज्ञानिनोऽत्यर्थमहं स च मम प्रियः ॥१७॥
उदाराः सर्व एवैते ज्ञानी त्वात्मैव मे मतम् ।
आस्थितः स हि युक्तात्मा मामेवानुत्तमां गतिम् ॥१८॥
बहूनां जन्मनामन्ते ज्ञानवान्मां प्रपद्यते ।
वासुदेवः सर्वमिति स महात्मा सुदुर्लभः ॥१९॥

कामैस्तैस्तैर्हृतज्ञानाः प्रपद्यन्तेऽन्यदेवताः ।
तं तं नियममास्थाय प्रकृत्या नियताः स्वया ॥२०॥
यो यो यां यां तनुं भक्तः श्रद्धयार्चितुमिच्छति ।
तस्य तस्याचलां श्रद्धां तामेव विदधाम्यहम् ॥२१॥
स तया श्रद्धया युक्तस्तस्याराधनमीहते ।
लभते च ततः कामान्मयैव विहितान्हितान् ॥२२॥
अन्तवत्तु फलं तेषां तद्भवत्यल्पमेधसाम् ।
देवान्देवयजो यान्ति मद्भक्ता यान्ति मामपि ॥२३॥

Four kinds of people do worship Me:
Those who want something,
those who are unhappy,
those who want to know the truth,
and those who are wise.
Of these four kinds of people, the best are the wise
because they love Me most.
Wise people love God with all their heart
and I love them back very much.
But only a very wise person after many many lives
realizes the truth: God is everything.

I let you worship and love Me
in any way you like, any way at all,
Because loving God is always good.
Loving God in every way, in every shape,
and with every name is good.

अव्यक्तं व्यक्तिमापन्नं मन्यन्ते मामबुद्धयः ।
परं भावमजानन्तो ममाव्ययमनुत्तमम् ॥२४॥
नाहं प्रकाशः सर्वस्य योगमायासमावृतः ।
मूढोऽयं नाभिजानाति लोको मामजमव्ययम् ॥२५॥
वेदाहं समतीतानि वर्तमानानि चार्जुन ।
भविष्याणि च भूतानि मां तु वेद न कश्चन ॥२६॥

इच्छाद्वेषसमुत्थेन द्वन्द्वमोहेन भारत ।
सर्वभूतानि संमोहं सर्गे यान्ति परंतप ॥२७॥

येषां त्वन्तगतं पापं जनानां पुण्यकर्मणाम् ।
ते द्वन्द्वमोहनिर्मुक्ता भजन्ते मां दृढव्रताः ॥२८॥
जरामरणमोक्षाय मामाश्रित्य यतन्ति ये ।
ते ब्रह्म तद्विदुः कृत्स्नमध्यात्मं कर्म चाखिलम् ॥२९॥
साधिभूताधिदैवं मां साधियज्ञं च ये विदुः ।
प्रयाणकालेऽपि च मां ते विदुर्युक्तचेतसः ॥३०॥

I know all beings,
past, present and future,
But they do not know Me.

Not all can see Me
because their minds
are covered by foolishness and desire.
They are confused by opposites,
like wanting and hating,
and their confusion covers up the truth
which is God.

Oh Arjun, people in the world do not understand Me.
But wise people,
the best people, keep trying to understand God.
And those who do not stop trying — ever —
finally know Me and My secret.

श्री

अथाष्टमोऽध्यायः

किं तद्ब्रह्म किमध्यात्मं किं कर्म पुरुषोत्तम ।
अधिभूतं च किं प्रोक्तमधिदैवं किमुच्यते ॥१॥
अधियज्ञः कथं कोऽत्र देहेऽस्मिन्मधुसूदन ।
प्रयाणकाले च कथं ज्ञेयोऽसि नियतात्मभिः ॥२॥
अक्षरं ब्रह्म परमं स्वभावोऽध्यात्ममुच्यते ।
भूतभावोद्भवकरो विसर्गः कर्मसंज्ञितः ॥३॥
अधिभूतं क्षरो भावः पुरुषश्चाधिदैवतम् ।
अधियज्ञोऽहमेवात्र देहे देहभृतां वर ॥४॥
अन्तकाले च मामेव स्मरन्मुक्त्वा कलेवरम् ।
यः प्रयाति स मद्भावं याति नास्त्यत्र संशयः ॥५॥
यंयं वापि स्मरन्भावं त्यजत्यन्ते कलेवरम् ।
तं तमेवैति कौन्तेय सदा तद्भावभावितः ॥६॥
तस्मात्सर्वेषु कालेषु मामनुस्मर युध्य च ।
मय्यर्पितमनोबुद्धिर्मामेवैष्यस्यसंशयम् ॥७॥
अभ्यासयोगयुक्तेन चेतसा नान्यगामिना ।
परमं पुरुषं दिव्यं याति पार्थानुचिन्तयन् ॥८॥

Chapter 8
Brahma

Arjun asked:

Lord Krishna, what is Brahma?

Bhagvan answered:

Brahma is the spirit of God.
It is everlasting
and the origin of all beings.
Those who die thinking of Me
come to Me and become everlasting.
So think of Me, Arjun,
and fight!

I am God,
the wise,
the everlasting ruler of all.

कविं पुराणमनुशासितार-
मणोरणीयांसमनुस्मरेद्यः ।
सर्वस्य धातारमचिन्त्यरूप-
मादित्यवर्णं तमसः परस्तात् ॥ ९ ॥
प्रयाणकाले मनसाचलेन
भक्त्या युक्तो योगबलेन चैव ।
भ्रुवोर्मध्ये प्राणमावेश्य सम्यक्
स तं परं पुरुषमुपैति दिव्यम् ॥१०॥
यदक्षरं वेदविदो वदन्ति विशन्ति यद्यतयो वीतरागाः ।
यदिच्छन्तो ब्रह्मचर्यं चरन्ति तत्ते पदं संग्रहेण प्रवक्ष्ये ॥११॥
सर्वद्वाराणि संयम्य मनो हृदि निरुध्य च ।
मूर्ध्न्याधायात्मनः प्राणमास्थितो योगधारणाम् ॥१२॥
ओमित्येकाक्षरं ब्रह्म व्याहरन्मामनुस्मरन् ।
यः प्रयाति त्यजन्देहं स याति परमां गतिम् ॥१३॥
अनन्यचेताः सततं यो मां स्मरति नित्यशः ।
तस्याहं सुलभः पार्थ नित्ययुक्तस्य योगिनः ॥१४॥
मामुपेत्य पुनर्जन्म दुःखालयमशाश्वतम् ।
नाप्नुवन्ति महात्मानः संसिद्धिं परमां गताः ॥१५॥
आब्रह्मभुवनाल्लोकाः पुनरावर्तिनोऽर्जुन ।
मामुपेत्य तु कौन्तेय पुनर्जन्म न विद्यते ॥१६॥
सहस्रयुगपर्यन्तमहर्यद्ब्रह्मणो विदुः ।
रात्रिं युगसहस्रान्तां तेऽहोरात्रविदो जनाः ॥१७॥

God is beyond what your mind can understand.
God shines like the sun
far beyond the darkness of ignorance.

Arjun, I will tell you more about God.
I can easily be reached
by those who think of Me all the time.
And if you reach Me,
you will not need to be born again
But you can stay with Me
forever and ever.

Brahma's day lasts a thousand ages
and Brahma's night lasts a thousand more.
Only the wise
know this truth
about Time.

अव्यक्ताद्व्यक्तयः सर्वाः प्रभवन्त्यहरागमे ।
रात्र्यागमे प्रलीयन्ते तत्रैवाव्यक्तसंज्ञके ॥१८॥
भूतग्रामः स एवायं भूत्वा भूत्वा प्रलीयते ।
रात्र्यागमेऽवशः पार्थ प्रभवत्यहरागमे ॥१९॥
परस्तस्मात्तु भावोऽन्योऽव्यक्तोऽव्यक्तात्सनातनः ।
यः स सर्वेषु भूतेषु नश्यत्सु न विनश्यति ॥२०॥
अव्यक्तोऽक्षर इत्युक्तस्तमाहुः परमां गतिम् ।
यं प्राप्य न निवर्तन्ते तद्धाम परमं मम ॥२१॥
पुरुषः स परः पार्थ भक्त्या लभ्यस्त्वनन्यया ।
यस्यान्तःस्थानि भूतानि येन सर्वमिदं ततम् ॥२२॥
यत्र काले त्वनावृत्तिमावृत्तिं चैव योगिनः ।
प्रयाता यान्ति तं कालं वक्ष्यामि भरतर्षभ ॥२३॥
अग्निर्ज्योतिरहः शुक्लः षण्मासा उत्तरायणम् ।
तत्र प्रयाता गच्छन्ति ब्रह्म ब्रह्मविदो जनाः ॥२४॥
धूमो रात्रिस्तथा कृष्णः षण्मासा दक्षिणायनम् ।
तत्र चान्द्रमसं ज्योतिर्योगी प्राप्य निवर्तते ॥२५॥
शुक्लकृष्णे गती ह्येते जगतः शाश्वते मते ।
एकया यात्यनावृत्तिमन्यया वर्तते पुनः ॥२६॥
नैते सृती पार्थ जानन्योगी मुह्यति कश्चन ।
तस्मात्सर्वेषु कालेषु योगयुक्तो भवार्जुन ॥२७॥
वेदेषु यज्ञेषु तपःसु चैव दानेषु यत्पुण्यफलं प्रदिष्टम् ।
अत्येति तत्सर्वमिदं विदित्वा योगी परं स्थानमुपैति चाद्यम् ॥२८॥

The world is born
when Brahma's day begins
and it disappears
when Brahma's night begins.
This happens over and over again.

But God is beyond this world
which appears and disappears.
God is everlasting.
Those who love Him completely
are also everlasting
and past this world of birth and death.

God is permanent.
He is not destroyed in the destruction of the world.
God is the best resting place
from which those who love Him do not have to return.

श्री

नवमोऽध्यायः

इदं तु ते गुह्यतमं प्रवक्ष्याम्यनसूयवे ।
ज्ञानं विज्ञानसहितं यज्ज्ञात्वा मोक्ष्यसेऽशुभात् ॥ १ ॥

राजविद्या राजगुह्यं पवित्रमिदमुत्तमम् ।
प्रत्यक्षावगमं धर्म्यं सुसुखं कर्तुमव्ययम् ॥ २ ॥

अश्रद्दधानाः पुरुषा धर्मस्यास्य परन्तप ।
अप्राप्य मां निवर्तन्ते मृत्युसंसारवर्त्मनि ॥ ३ ॥

मया ततमिदं सर्वं जगदव्यक्तमूर्तिना ।
मत्स्थानि सर्वभूतानि न चाहं तेष्ववस्थितः ॥ ४ ॥

Chapter 9

The Holy Secret

Bhagvan said:

To you,

I will give the holy secret

which will keep everything bad

away from you.

This secret is the best, the loveliest, the holiest.

It is a wonderful, everlasting secret.

The world is filled with Me, God,

like a room is filled with air.

This is how I am not really a part of people,

but I am everywhere and they are in Me.

न च मत्स्थानि भूतानि पश्य मे योगमैश्वरम् ।
भूतभृन्न च भूतस्थो ममात्मा भूतभावनः ॥ ५ ॥

यथाऽकाशस्थितो नित्यं वायुः सर्वत्रगो महान् ।
तथा सर्वाणि भूतानि मत्स्थानीत्युपधारय ॥ ६ ॥

सर्वभूतानि कौन्तेय प्रकृतिं यान्ति मामिकाम् ।
कल्पक्षये पुनस्तानि कल्पादौ विसृजाम्यहम् ॥ ७ ॥

प्रकृतिं स्वामवष्टभ्य विसृजामि पुनः पुनः ।
भूतग्राममिमं कृत्स्नमवशः प्रकृतेर्वशात् ॥ ८ ॥

न च मां तानि कर्माणि निबध्नन्ति धनञ्जय ।
उदासीनवदासीनमसक्तं तेषु कर्मसु ॥ ९ ॥

मयाऽध्यक्षेण प्रकृतिः सूयते सचराचरम् ।
हेतुनाऽनेन कौन्तेय जगद्विपरिवर्तते ॥ १० ॥

The whole world was My idea
and was born from Me.

Arjun, at the end of the world,
all living things get lost in Me
and then at the beginning of the world
everything is born again.
Nature begins again and the world becomes alive.

A great wheel makes the world turn round and round
and it makes the world get lost in God
and get born again.

The world disappears and reappears like this
many times
because I want it to.

अवजानन्ति मां मूढा मानुषीं तनुमाश्रितम् ।
परं भावमजानन्तो मम भूतमहेश्वरम् ॥११॥

मोघाशा मोघकर्माणो मोघज्ञाना विचेतसः ।
राक्षसीमासुरीं चैव प्रकृतिं मोहिनीं श्रिताः ॥१२॥

❁

महात्मानस्तु मां पार्थ दैवीं प्रकृतिमाश्रिताः ।
भजन्त्यनन्यमनसो ज्ञात्वा भूतादिमव्ययम् ॥१३॥

सततं कीर्तयन्तो मां यतन्तश्च दृढव्रताः ।
नमस्यन्तश्च मां भक्त्या नित्ययुक्ता उपासते ॥१४॥

❁

ज्ञानयज्ञेन चाप्यन्ये यजन्तो मामुपासते ।
एकत्वेन पृथक्त्वेन बहुधा विश्वतोमुखम् ॥१५॥

अहं क्रतुरहं यज्ञः स्वधाहमहमौषधम् ।
मन्त्रोऽहमहमेवाज्यमहमग्निरहं हुतम् ॥१६॥

Fools don't recognize God.
They are silly and unhappy.
They think I am just a man.
But good and wise people know Me.
They know I make the world and they worship Me.
Good people call out My name
and bow to Me,
and pray to Me
and think of Me all the time.

Good people love Me in different ways.
These ways are studying about God
and thinking about God and My many names
and My many forms.
I am prayers, and pujas, and ghee,
and sweets and the holy fire.

पिताऽहमस्य जगतो माता धाता पितामहः ।
वेद्यं पवित्रमोंकार ऋक् साम यजुरेव च ॥१७॥
गतिर्भर्ता प्रभुः साक्षी निवासः शरणं सुहृत् ।
प्रभवः प्रलयः स्थानं निधानं बीजमव्ययम् ॥१८॥

तपाम्यहमहं वर्षं निगृह्णाम्युत्सृजामि च ।
अमृतं चैव मृत्युश्च सदसच्चाहमर्जुन ॥१९॥

त्रैविद्या मां सोमपाः पूतपापा
यज्ञैरिष्ट्वा स्वर्गतिं पार्थयन्ते ।
ते पुण्यमासाद्य सुरेन्द्रलोक-
मश्नन्ति दिव्यान्दिवि देवभोगान् ॥२०॥
ते तं भुक्त्वा स्वर्गलोकं विशालं
क्षीणे पुण्ये मर्त्यलोकं विशन्ति ।
एवं त्रयीधर्ममनुप्रपन्ना
गतागतं कामकामा लभन्ते ॥२१॥

I am the King of the Universe.
I am its Father and Mother and Grandfather.
I am making things and I am taking things apart.
I am the beginning and the end.
I am being born and dying
and I am living forever.

I am the heat in the sun
and the water in the rain.
I cause and I hold back showers.

People who pray to Me
because they want something,
go to heaven and rejoice there.
But then they are born again
and they die again.

अनन्याश्चिन्तयन्तो मां ये जनाः पर्युपासते ।
तेषां नित्याभियुक्तानां योगक्षेमं वहाम्यहम् ॥२२॥

येऽप्यन्यदेवता भक्ता यजन्ते श्रद्धयान्विताः ।
तेऽपि मामेव कौन्तेय यजन्त्यविधिपूर्वकम् ॥२३॥

अहं हि सर्वयज्ञानां भोक्ता च प्रभुरेव च ।
न तु मामभिजानन्ति तत्त्वेनातश्च्यवन्ति ते ॥२४॥

यान्ति देवव्रता देवान् पितॄन्यान्ति पितृव्रताः ।
भूतानि यान्ति भूतेज्या यान्ति मद्याजिनोऽपि माम् ॥२५॥

पत्रं पुष्पं फलं तोयं यो मे भक्त्या प्रयच्छति ।
तदहं भक्त्युपहृतमश्नामि प्रयतात्मनः ॥२६॥

यत्करोषि यदश्नासि यज्जुहोषि ददासि यत् ।
यत्तपस्यसि कौन्तेय तत्कुरुष्व मदर्पणम् ॥२७॥

शुभाशुभफलैरेवं मोक्ष्यसे कर्मबन्धनैः ।
संन्यासयोगयुक्तात्मा विमुक्तो मामुपैष्यसि ॥२८॥

But people who pray just because they love Me,
not because they want something, are the best
and I take care of them forever.

If a person gives Me a leaf, a flower,
a fruit, or even just water,
the person sees Me in his mind.
I come and happily take whatever he gives Me
with love.

Arjun, whatever you do, whatever you eat,
whatever you give Me as a gift,
do it, and eat it and give it for Me.
If you are sorry, punish yourself for Me too.
If you do everything for My sake,
instead of for yourself,
You will do everything good and come right to Me.

समोऽहं सर्वभूतेषु न मे द्वेष्योऽस्ति न प्रियः ।
ये भजन्ति तु मां भक्त्या मयि ते तेषु चाप्यहम् ॥२९॥

अपि चेत्सुदुराचारो भजते मामनन्यभाक् ।
साधुरेव स मन्तव्यः सम्यग्व्यवसितो हि सः ॥३०॥

क्षिप्रं भवति धर्मात्मा शश्वच्छान्तिं निगच्छति ।
कौन्तेय प्रतिजानीहि न मे भक्तः प्रणश्यति ॥३१॥

मां हि पार्थ व्यपाश्रित्य येऽपि स्युः पापयोनयः ।
स्त्रियो वैश्यास्तथा शूद्रास्तेऽपि यान्ति परांगतिम् ॥३२॥

किं पुनर्ब्राह्मणाः पुण्या भक्ता राजर्षयस्तथा ।
अनित्यमसुखं लोकमिमं प्राप्य भजस्व माम् ॥३३॥

मन्मना भव मद्भक्तो मद्याजी मां नमस्कुरु ।
मामेवैष्यसि युक्त्वैवमात्मानं मत्परायणः ॥३४॥

I am everywhere.
I do not hate or love.
But the persons who worship Me
live in God and can recognize God in themselves.

Even the worst people, even sinners, are good
if they love Me with all their heart.
They become good very quickly
and become happy forever.
Oh Arjun, you can be sure that this is true.
Everyone who loves Me becomes happy.

The holy secret is this:
By loving God, Me,
you can come right up to God.
Thinking of God, loving God,
bowing to God, joining God
and trusting God is the way to God.

श्री

दशमोऽध्यायः

भूय एव महाबाहो शृणु मे परमं वचः ।
यत्तेऽहं प्रीयमाणाय वक्ष्यामि हितकाम्यया ॥ १ ॥

न मे विदुः सुरगणाः प्रभवं न महर्षयः ।
अहमादिर्हि देवानां महर्षीणां च सर्वशः ॥ २ ॥

यो मामजमनादिं च वेत्ति लोकमहेश्वरम् ।
असंमूढः स मर्त्येषु सर्वपापैः प्रमुच्यते ॥ ३ ॥

Chapter 10

God's Glories

Bhagvan said:

Arjun, listen to Me again.

I talk to you because you love Me.

I talk to you for your own good.

No one knows the secret of My power.

Not even the wisest people

know the secret of My origin.

I, God,

am the cause of everything in the universe.

I am God, the Lord of the world.

I have no birth and no beginning.

People who know this are good.

बुद्धिर्ज्ञानमसंमोहः क्षमा सत्यं दमः शमः ।
सुखं दुःखं भवोऽभावो भयं चाभयमेव च ॥ ४ ॥

अहिंसा समता तुष्टिस्तपो दानं यशोऽयशः ।
भवन्ति भावा भूतानां मत्त एव पृथग्विधाः ॥ ५ ॥

महर्षयः सप्त पूर्वे चत्वारो मनवस्तथा ।
मद्भावा मानसा जाता येषां लोक इमाः प्रजाः ॥ ६ ॥

एतां विभूतिं योगं च मम यो वेत्ति तत्त्वतः ।
सोऽविकम्पेन योगेन युज्यते नात्र संशयः ॥ ७ ॥

अहं सर्वस्य प्रभवो मत्तः सर्वं प्रवर्तते ।
इति मत्वा भजन्ते मां बुधा भावसमन्विताः ॥ ८ ॥

मच्चित्ता मद्गतप्राणा बोधयन्तः परस्परम् ।
कथयन्तश्च मां नित्यं तुष्यन्ति च रमन्ति च ॥ ९ ॥

Everything comes from Me, only from Me.
Truth, wisdom, forgiveness, self control,
happiness, unhappiness, bravery, fear,
peacefulness, fame and shame
all come from God.

All the great makers of the world were born
because I wanted them to be.
I started the world.
The world moves because of Me.
Wise, good people worship Me
because they know this.

The wise think of Me;
give up their lives to Me;
tell each other about God
and are happy because of Me.

तेषां सततयुक्तानां भजतां प्रीतिपूर्वकम् ।
ददामि बुद्धियोगं तं येन मामुपयान्ति ते ॥१०॥
तेषामेवानुकम्पार्थमहमज्ञानजं तमः ।
नाशयाम्यात्मभावस्थो ज्ञानदीपेन भास्वता ॥११॥
परं ब्रह्म परं धाम पवित्रं परमं भवान् ।
पुरुषं शाश्वतं दिव्यमादिदेवमजं विभुम् ॥१२॥
आहुस्त्वामृषयः सर्वे देवर्षिर्नारदस्तथा ।
असितो देवलो व्यासः स्वयं चैव ब्रवीषि मे ॥१३॥

सर्वमेतदृतं मन्ये यन्मां वदसि केशव ।
न हि ते भगवन्व्यक्तिं विदुर्देवा न दानवाः ॥१४॥

स्वयमेवात्मनात्मानं वेत्थ त्वं पुरुषोत्तम ।
भूतभावन भूतेश देवदेव जगत्पते ॥१५॥
वक्तुमर्हस्यशेषेण दिव्या ह्यात्मविभूतयः ।
याभिर्विभूतिभिर्लोकानिमांस्त्वं व्याप्य तिष्ठसि ॥१६॥
कथं विद्यामहं योगिंस्त्वां सदा परिचिन्तयन् ।
केषु केषु च भावेषु चिन्त्योऽसि भगवन्मया ॥१७॥
विस्तरेणात्मनो योगं विभूतिं च जनार्दन ।
भूयः कथय तृप्तिर्हि शृण्वतो नास्ति मेऽमृतम् ॥१८॥

I love those who worship Me
and I give them wisdom.
I live in their heart
and push away darkness
and shine the light of truth on them.

Arjun said to God:
You are the great everlasting God.
Saints say You are God and You are blessing me
by telling me all about Yourself.

Krishna,
I believe everything You tell me.

Oh Lord, how can I know You?
How can I pray to You?
How can I imagine You?

हन्त ते कथयिष्यामि दिव्या ह्यात्मविभूतयः ।
प्राधान्यतः कुरुश्रेष्ठ नास्त्यन्तो विस्तरस्य मे ॥१९॥

ॐ

अहमात्मा गुडाकेश सर्वभूताशयस्थितः ।
अहमादिश्च मध्यं च भूतानामन्त एव च ॥२०॥

ॐ

आदित्यानामहं विष्णुर्ज्योतिषां रविरंशुमान् ।
मरीचिर्मरुतामस्मि नक्षत्राणामहं शशी ॥२१॥

ॐ

Please Krishna,

tell me again exactly

about Your strength and about Your glory

because I can never stop wishing

to hear more about You, Oh God.

Bhagvan said:

Arjun, I will tell you more about my glories.

They are endless.

Oh Arjun,

I am in the heart of all living things.

I am their beginning, their middle, and their end.

I am Vishnu.

I am the sun and the wind.

I am the moon.

वेदानां सामवेदोऽस्मि देवानामस्मि वासवः ।
इन्द्रियाणां मनश्चास्मि भूतानामस्मि चेतना ॥२२॥
रुद्राणां शंकरश्चास्मि वित्तेशो यक्षरक्षसाम् ।
वसूनां पावकश्चास्मि मेरुः शिखरिणामहम् ॥२३॥
पुरोधसां च मुख्यं मां विद्धि पार्थ बृहस्पतिम् ।
सेनानीनामहं स्कन्दः सरसामस्मि सागरः ॥२४॥

महर्षीणां भृगुरहं गिरामस्म्येकमक्षरम् ।
यज्ञानां जपयज्ञोऽस्मि स्थावराणां हिमालयः ॥२५॥
अश्वत्थः सर्ववृक्षाणां देवर्षीणां च नारदः ।
गन्धर्वाणां चित्ररथः सिद्धानां कपिलो मुनिः ॥२६॥
उच्चैःश्रवसमश्वानां विद्धि माममृतोद्भवम् ।
ऐरावतं गजेन्द्राणां नराणां च नराधिपम् ॥२७॥

I am Indra.

I am the mind.

I am energy.

I am what destroys things. I am richness.

I am fire. I am the tallest of mountains.

I am the chief priest and the strongest general.

I am the ocean. I am a mind reader. I am Om.

I am the holiest of trees, the musician of heaven,

the wisest of men.

I am the horse that was born

when the ocean was mixed with honey.

I am the white elephant.

I am the King.

आयुधानामहं वज्रं धेनूनामस्मि कामधुक् ।
प्रजनश्चास्मि कन्दर्पः सर्पाणामस्मि वासुकिः ॥२८॥
अनन्तश्चास्मि नागानां वरुणो यादसामहम् ।
पितॄणामर्यमा चास्मि यमः संयमतामहम् ॥२९॥
प्रह्लादश्चास्मि दैत्यानां कालः कलयतामहम् ।
मृगाणां च मृगेन्द्रोऽहं वैनतेयश्च पक्षिणाम् ॥३०॥

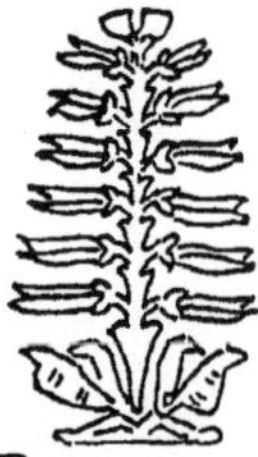

पवनः पवतामस्मि रामः शस्त्रभृतामहम् ।
झषाणां मकरश्चास्मि स्रोतसामस्मि जाह्नवी ॥३१॥

सर्गाणामादिरन्तश्च मध्यं चैवाहमर्जुन ।
अध्यात्मविद्या विद्यानां वादः प्रवदतामहम् ॥३२॥
अक्षराणामकारोऽस्मि द्वन्द्वः सामासिकस्य च ।
अहमेवाक्षयः कालो धाताऽहं विश्वतोमुखः ॥३३॥
मृत्युः सर्वहरश्चाहमुद्भवश्च भविष्यताम् ।
कीर्तिः श्रीर्वाक् च नारीणां स्मृतिर्मेधा धृतिः क्षमा ॥३४॥

Of weapons, I am the most powerful thunderbolt.
I am the heavenly cow.
I make men and women
love each other and have children.

I am the snake god and the water god.
I am Yama, the god of death. I am Time.

Of beasts, I am the lion
and of birds, I am Garuda on whom Lord Vishnu rides.

I am the wind that purifies the air. I am Rama.

I am the alligator. Of rivers, I am the holy Ganges.
I am the letter A. I keep the world alive.
My face is on all sides.
And I am death.
And I am the future.

बृहत्साम तथा साम्नां गायत्री छन्दसामहम् ।
मासानां मार्गशीर्षोऽहमृतूनां कुसुमाकरः ॥३५॥

द्यूतं छलयतामस्मि तेजस्तेजस्विनामहम् ।
जयोऽस्मि व्यवसायोऽस्मि सत्त्वं सत्त्ववतामहम् ॥३६॥

वृष्णीनां वासुदेवोऽस्मि पाण्डवानां धनञ्जयः ।
मुनीनामप्यहं व्यासः कवीनामुशना कविः ॥३७॥

दण्डो दमयतामस्मि नीतिरस्मि जिगीषताम् ।
मौनं चैवास्मि गुह्यानां ज्ञानं ज्ञानवतामहम् ॥३८॥

यच्चापि सर्वभूतानां बीजं तदहमर्जुन ।
न तदस्ति विना यत्स्यान्मया भूतं चराचरम् ॥३९॥

नान्तोऽस्ति मम दिव्यानां विभूतीनां परन्तप ।
एष तूद्देशतः प्रोक्तो विभूतेर्विस्तरो मया ॥४०॥

I am the feminine qualities of fame,
richness, speech, memory, smartness,
steadiness and forgiveness.

I am divine songs and verses.
I am spring.
I am victory and I am the goodness in all that is good.
I am you, Arjun, of the Pandavas.

I am the secret keeper.
I am Truth in those who know.
I am the seed of everything.
Nothing alive or lifeless exists without Me.

Oh Arjun, there is no end to all that I am.
There is no end to My divine forms.

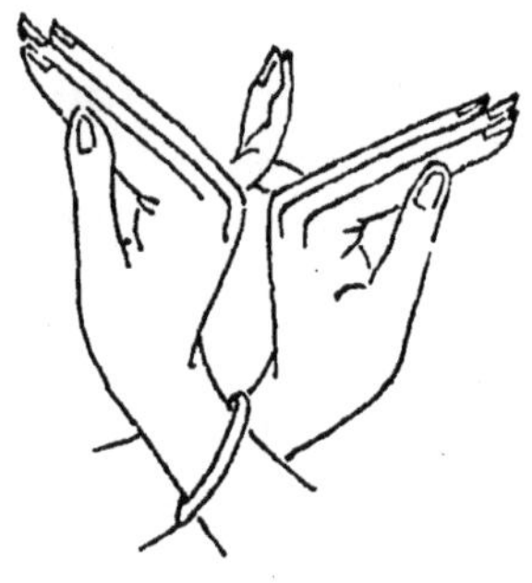

यद्यद्विभूतिमत्सत्त्वं श्रीमदूर्जितमेव वा ।
तत्तदेवावगच्छ त्वं मम तेजोंऽशसम्भवम् ॥४१॥

अथवा बहुनैतेन किं ज्ञातेन तवार्जुन ।
विष्टभ्याहमिदं कृत्स्नमेकांशेन स्थितो जगत् ॥४२॥

Everything

that is glorious or brilliant or strong

is a spark of My brightness.

I stand and hold the whole world

by just a spark of My magic.

श्री

अथैकादशोऽध्यायः

मदनुग्रहाय परमं गुह्यमध्यात्मसंज्ञितम् ।
यत्त्वयोक्तं वचस्तेन मोहोऽयं विगतो मम ॥ १ ॥

भवाप्ययो हि भूतानां श्रुतौ विस्तरशो मया ।
त्वत्तः कमलपत्राक्ष माहात्म्यमपि चाव्ययम् ॥ २ ॥

एवमेतद्यथात्थ त्वमात्मानं परमेश्वर ।
द्रष्टुमिच्छामि ते रूपमैश्वरं पुरुषोत्तम ॥ ३ ॥

मन्यसे यदि तच्छक्यं मया द्रष्टुमिति प्रभो ।
योगेश्वर ततो मे त्वं दर्शयात्मानमव्ययम् ॥ ४ ॥

Chapter 11

God Shows Himself to Arjun

Arjun said:

Thank you God for your secret words.

Thank you for your goodness to me.

Now all my mistakes have disappeared

because I have heard the truth from You.

Oh Lord,

You are all that You tell me.

But I am longing to see You.

Oh God, Oh Krishna,

if You think I am good enough to see how You look,

Oh God,

show Yourself to me.

पश्य मे पार्थ रूपाणि शतशोऽथ सहस्रशः ।
नानाविधानि दिव्यानि नानावर्णाकृतीनि च ॥ ५ ॥

पश्यादित्यान्वसून्रुद्रानश्विनौ मरुतस्तथा ।
बहून्यदृष्टपूर्वाणि पश्याश्चर्याणि भारत ॥ ६ ॥

इहैकस्थं जगत्कृत्स्नं पश्याद्य सचराचरम् ।
मम देहे गुडाकेश यच्चान्यद्द्रष्टुमिच्छसि ॥ ७ ॥

न तु मां शक्यसे द्रष्टुमनेनैव स्वचक्षुषा ।
दिव्यं ददामि ते चक्षुः पश्य मे योगमैश्वरम् ॥ ८ ॥

Bhagvan said:
Look! I am in hundreds of thousands
of different forms, and colors, and shapes.

See in Me all twelve sons of Aditi,
the eight Vasus, the eleven Rudras
who are gods of destruction, the twins
who are the gods' doctors, the forty-nine
wind gods, and many many other
wonderful forms never seen before.

Arjun, see in My body, the whole world
and anything else you want to see.

You cannot see Me with your human eyes
so I will give you a divine heavenly eye.
With it you will see My power and My greatness.

एवमुक्त्वा ततो राजन् महायोगेश्वरो हरिः ।
दर्शयामास पार्थाय परमं रूपमैश्वरम् ॥ ९॥

अनेकवक्त्रनयनमनेकाद्भुतदर्शनम् ।
अनेकदिव्याभरणं दिव्यानेकोद्यतायुधम् ॥१०॥

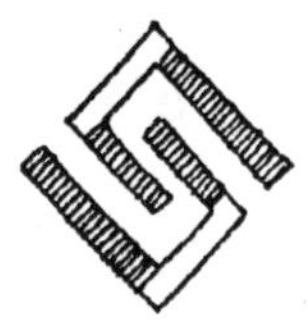

दिव्यमाल्याम्बरधरं दिव्यगन्धानुलेपनम् ।
सर्वाश्चर्यमयं देवमनन्तं विश्वतोमुखम् ॥११॥

दिवि सूर्यसहस्रस्य भवेद्युगपदुत्थिता ।
यदि भाः सदृशी सा स्याद्भासस्तस्य महात्मनः ॥१२॥

तत्रैकस्थं जगत्कृत्स्नं प्रविभक्तमनेकधा ।
अपश्यद्देवदेवस्य शरीरे पाण्डवस्तदा ॥१३॥

Sanjay said:
After saying this,
Krishna showed Arjun His divine universal form.

Arjun saw God with many mouths and eyes,
a wonderful sight, with divine jewels
and weapons,
and heavenly garlands
and clothes,
and covered with fragrant paste, full of wonder, endless,
and having faces on all sides.

The glow of a thousand suns
all shining together in the sky
would hardly be as bright as the shine of God.

ततः स विस्मयाविष्टो हृष्टरोमा धनञ्जयः ।
प्रणम्य शिरसा देवं कृताञ्जलिरभाषत ॥१४॥

पश्यामि देवांस्तव देव देहे
सर्वांस्तथा भूतविशेषसङ्घान् ।
ब्रह्माणमीशं कमलासनस्थ-
मृषींश्च सर्वानुरगांश्च दिव्यान् ॥१५॥

अनेकबाहूदरवक्त्रनेत्रं
पश्यामि त्वां सर्वतोऽनन्तरूपम् ।
नान्तं न मध्यं न पुनस्तवादिं
पश्यामि विश्वेश्वर विश्वरूप ॥१६॥

Then Arjun saw in God the whole universe.
Then Arjun, full of wonder,
with his hairs standing on end,
bowed down to the Lord
and pressing his hands in prayer said:

Oh Lord,
I see all the gods and thousands of beings in You:
Brahma sitting on his lotus;
Siva, and the wise men;
and heavenly serpents.

Oh God of the Universe,
I see You with many arms, many bellies,
many faces and many eyes.
Oh Lord,
I cannot see Your beginning or Your middle
or Your end.

किरीटिनं गदिनं चक्रिणं च
तेजोराशिं सर्वतो दीप्तिमन्तम् ।
पश्यामि त्वां दुर्निरीक्ष्यं समन्ता-
द्दीप्तानलार्कद्युतिमप्रमेयम् ॥१७॥

त्वमक्षरं परमं वेदितव्यं
त्वमस्य विश्वस्य परं निधानम् ।
त्वमव्ययः शाश्वतधर्मगोप्ता
सनातनस्त्वं पुरुषो मतो मे ॥१८॥

अनादिमध्यान्तमनन्तवीर्य-
मनन्तबाहुं शशिसूर्यनेत्रम् ।
पश्यामि त्वां दीप्तहुताशवक्त्रं
स्वतेजसा विश्वमिदं तपन्तम् ॥१९॥

द्यावापृथिव्योरिदमन्तरं हि
व्याप्तं त्वयैकेन दिशश्च सर्वाः ।
दृष्ट्वाद्भुतं रूपमुग्रं तवेदं
लोकत्रयं प्रव्यथितं महात्मन् ॥२०॥

I see You with a crown, a club, a chakra,
all round and bright like the fire and sun,
shining on all sides.

You are the protector of goodness.
You never end.

I see You with no beginning, no middle and no end,
with unending power and countless hands,
with the moon and sun for eyes,
and fire for Your mouth burning the world
with Your brightness.

The space between heaven and earth
is filled only by You.
Oh Lord, seeing this wonderful and terrible form
of You, God, all these worlds are frightened.

अमी हि त्वां सुरसंघा विशन्ति
केचिद्भीताः प्राञ्जलयो गृणन्ति ।
स्वस्तीत्युक्त्वा महर्षिसिद्धसंघाः
स्तुवन्ति त्वां स्तुतिभिः पुष्कलाभिः ॥२१॥

ॐ

रुद्रादित्या वसवो येच साध्या
विश्वेऽश्विनौ मरुतश्चोष्मपाश्च ।
गन्धर्वयक्षासुरसिद्धसंघा
वीक्षन्ते त्वां विस्मिताश्चैव सर्वे ॥२२॥
रूपं महत्ते बहुवक्त्रनेत्रं
महाबाहो बहुबाहूरुपादम् ।
बहूदरं बहुदंष्ट्राकरालं
दृष्ट्वा लोकाः प्रव्यथितास्तथाहम् ॥२३॥
नभःस्पृशं दीप्तमनेकवर्णं
व्यात्ताननं दीप्तविशालनेत्रम् ।
दृष्ट्वा हि त्वां प्रव्यथितान्तरात्मा
धृतिं न विन्दामि शमं च विष्णो ॥२४॥
दंष्ट्राकरालानि च ते मुखानि
दृष्ट्वैव कालानलसन्निभानि ।
दिशो न जाने न लभे च शर्म
प्रसीद देवेश जगन्निवास ॥२५॥

Crowds of divine forms are entering You;
some with joined hands are calling out
Your names and glories.
Some are saying "Let there be peace"
and praising You.
All are looking at You and are amazed.

Lord, the worlds are afraid,
seeing all Your faces and eyes
and arms and legs and bellies and teeth,
and so am I.

Arjun went on:
Your many colored forms and wide open mouth
and large shining eyes frighten me.
Your faces with terrible teeth
like fire burning the world frighten me.

अमी च त्वां धृतराष्ट्रस्य पुत्राः
सर्वे सहैवावनिपालसंघैः ।
भीष्मो द्रोणः सूतपुत्रस्तथासौ
सहास्मदीयैरपि योधमुख्यैः ॥२६॥
वक्त्राणि ते त्वरमाणा विशन्ति
दंष्ट्राकरालानि भयानकानि ।
केचिद्विलग्ना दशनान्तरेषु
संदृश्यन्ते चूर्णितैरुत्तमाङ्गैः ॥२७॥
यथा नदीनां बहवोऽम्बुवेगाः
समुद्रमेवाभिमुखा द्रवन्ति ।
तथा तवामी नरलोकवीरा
विशन्ति वक्त्राण्यभिविज्वलन्ति ॥२८॥
यथा प्रदीप्तं ज्वलनं पतङ्गा
विशन्ति नाशाय समृद्धवेगाः ।
तथैव नाशाय विशन्ति लोका
स्तवापि वक्त्राणि समृद्धवेगाः ॥२९॥

लेलिह्यसे ग्रसमानः समन्ता
ल्लोकान्समग्रान्वदनैर्ज्वलद्भिः ।
तेजोभिरापूर्य जगत्समग्रं
भासस्तवोग्राः प्रतपन्ति विष्णो ॥३०॥

Bhishma, Drona, and Karna with some of our warriors
are entering You.
All the sons of Dhritarashtra with kings and warriors
are entering You.
They are rushing
into Your fearful mouth with terrible teeth.
Some are stuck between Your teeth
with their heads smashed.
Like the rivers rush into the sea,
so these warriors are rushing into Your burning mouths.
They are going to be destroyed
like moths rushing into a fire.
Oh God,
You are swallowing through Your burning mouths.
You are licking all those people.
Your terrible brightness is burning the whole world,
filling it with light.

आख्याहि मे को भवानुग्ररूपो
नमोऽस्तु ते देववर प्रसीद ।
विज्ञातुमिच्छामि भवन्तमाद्यं
न हि प्रजानामि तव प्रवृत्तिम् ॥३१॥

कालोऽस्मि लोकक्षयकृत्प्रवृद्धो
लोकान्समाहर्तुमिह प्रवृत्तः ।
ऋतेऽपि त्वां न भविष्यन्ति सर्वे
येऽवस्थिताः प्रत्यनीकेषु योधाः ॥३२॥

तस्मात्त्वमुत्तिष्ठ यशो लभस्व
जित्वा शत्रून्भुङ्क्ष्व राज्यं समृद्धम् ।
मयैवैते निहताः पूर्वमेव
निमित्तमात्रं भव सव्यसाचिन् ॥३३॥

Lord, tell me who You are, looking so terrible!
I bow down to You. Be kind, Oh God!
I wish to know You because I do not understand
the reason for Your frightening form.

Bhagvan said:
I am burning Time, the destroyer of the world.
My reason now is to destroy these armies.
All your enemies will not live, Arjun,
even though you yourself do not kill them.

So arise, fight and win glory!
Enjoy victory.
These warriors, your enemies, will be killed by Me,
God, not by you.
I am just using you, Arjun, to destroy them.

द्रोणं च भीष्मं च जयद्रथं च
कर्णं तथान्यानपि योधवीरान् ।
मया हतांस्त्वं जहि माव्यथिष्ठा
युध्यस्व जेतासि रणे सपत्नान् ॥३४॥

एतच्छ्रुत्वा वचनं केशवस्य
कृताञ्जलिर्वेपमानः किरीटी ।
नमस्कृत्वा भूय एवाह कृष्णं
सगद्गदं भीतभीतः प्रणम्य ॥३५॥

स्थाने हृषीकेश तव प्रकीर्त्या
जगत्प्रहृष्यत्यनुरज्यते च ।
रक्षांसि भीतानि दिशो द्रवन्ति
सर्वे नमस्यन्ति च सिद्धसंघाः ॥३६॥

Kill Drona and Bhishma and Karna and others
who are already killed by Me.
You will be sure to conquer your enemies and win,
so fight!

Sanjay said:
Hearing these words of Bhagvan,
Arjun trembled and bowed down
and spoke in a very frightened and shaky voice.

Arjun said:
It is right, Oh God, that the world rejoices
and is filled with love by singing
Your names and glory.
Frightened demons are running away
and the saints are bowing to You.

कस्माच्च ते न नमेरन्महात्मन्
गरीयसे ब्रह्मणोऽप्यादिकर्त्रे ।
अनन्त देवेश जगन्निवास
त्वमक्षरं सदसत्तत्परं यत् ॥३७॥

त्वमादिदेवः पुरुषः पुराण-
स्त्वमस्य विश्वस्य परं निधानम् ।
वेत्तासि वेद्यं च परं च धाम
त्वया ततं विश्वमनन्तरूप ॥३८॥

वायुर्यमोऽग्निर्वरुणः शशाङ्कः
प्रजापतिस्त्वं प्रपितामहश्च ।
नमो नमस्तेऽस्तु सहस्रकृत्वः
पुनश्च भूयोऽपि नमो नमस्ते ॥३९॥

Oh God, they bow to You

because You are the greatest of the great.

You are the Lord of Heaven.

You are Sat, what is real.

You are Asat, what is not real.

And You are beyond both.

You are the main God, the oldest God.

You know; You are the knowable.

You fill the whole world in different shapes.

You are the wind god, Vayu;

the god of death, Yama; and the fire god, Agni.

You are the moon god.

You are Brahma, the Creator.

Indeed,

You are the father of Brahma, the Creator.

नमः पुरस्तादथ पृष्ठतस्ते
नमोऽस्तु ते सर्वत एव सर्व ।
अनन्तवीर्यामितविक्रमस्त्वं
सर्वं समाप्नोषि ततोऽसि सर्वः ॥४०॥

सखेति मत्वा प्रसभं यदुक्तं
हे कृष्ण हे यादव हे सखेति ।
अजानता महिमानं तवेदं
मया प्रमादात्प्रणयेन चापि ॥४१॥

यच्चावहासार्थमसत्कृतोऽसि
बिहारशय्यासनभोजनेषु ।
एकोऽथवाप्यच्युत तत्समक्षं
तत्क्षामये त्वामहमप्रमेयम् ॥४२॥

I bow to You.

I bow to You a thousand times.

I salute You and I salute You again and again.

Oh Lord of endless strength,

I salute You from all sides.

I salute You who have endless power,

who fill everything.

You are all.

Oh God,

I did not realize Your greatness.

I thought of You only as a friend.

I treated You as a friend.

Oh God, I beg You to forgive me.

Please God, You are perfect.

Forgive me!

पितासि लोकस्य चराचरस्य
त्वमस्य पूज्यश्च गुरुर्गरीयान् ।
न त्वत्समोऽस्त्यभ्यधिकः कुतोऽन्यो
लोकत्रयेऽप्यप्रतिमप्रभाव ॥४३॥

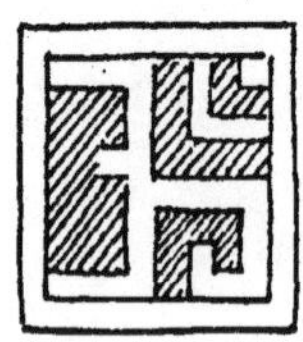

तस्मात्प्रणम्य प्रणिधाय कायं
प्रसादये त्वामहमीशमीड्यम् ।
पितेव पुत्रस्य सखेव सख्युः
प्रियः प्रियायार्हसि देव सोढुम् ॥४४॥

अदृष्टपूर्वं हृषितोऽस्मि दृष्ट्वा
भयेन च प्रव्यथितं मनो मे ।
तदेव मे दर्शय देव रूपं
प्रसीद देवेश जगन्निवास ॥४५॥

You are the father and also the greatest teacher.
No one can be as great as you.
How can anyone be greater?

So, Oh Lord, I bow at your feet and bow low.
I want to please You, the ruler of all.
Please forgive my mistake.
Forgive me like a father forgives his son,
like a friend forgives his friend,
and like a lover forgives his beloved.

After seeing what was unseen before,
I feel happy.
At the same time, my mind is afraid.
Please show me again
Your divine form of Vishnu with four arms,
Oh Lord.

किरीटिनं गदिनं चक्रहस्त-
मिच्छामि त्वां द्रष्टुमहं तथैव ।
तेनैव रूपेण चतुर्भुजेन
सहस्रबाहो भव विश्वमूर्ते ॥४६॥

मया प्रसन्नेन तवार्जुनेदं
रूपं परं दर्शितमात्मयोगात् ।
तेजोमयं विश्वमनन्तमाद्यं
यन्मे त्वदन्येन न दृष्टपूर्वम् ॥४७॥

न वेदयज्ञाध्ययनैर्न दानै-
र्न च क्रियाभिर्न तपोभिरुग्रैः ।
एवंरूपः शक्य अहं नृलोके
द्रष्टुं त्वदन्येन कुरुप्रवीर ॥४८॥

मा ते व्यथा मा च विमूढभावो
दृष्ट्वा रूपं घोरमीदृङ्ममेदम् ।
व्यपेतभीः प्रीतमनाः पुनस्त्वं
तदेव मे रूपमिदं प्रपश्य ॥४९॥

I wish to see You again with a crown, and a club
and a chakra wheel in Your hands.
Oh God with a thousand arms,
appear again in Your calm four armed form.

Bhagvan said:
Arjun, I am happy with you
so I have shown you my Universal form
which no one before has ever seen.
Arjun, in this world
no one except you can see Me like this.

Oh Arjun, do not worry or feel afraid
from seeing this terrible form of Mine.
Feel calm and unafraid.
Look, see Me again in my same four armed form,
with the conch, the chakra, the club, and the lotus.

इत्यर्जुनं वासुदेवस्तथोक्त्वा
स्वकं रूपं दर्शयामास भूयः ।
आश्वासयामास च भीतमेनं
भूत्वा पुनः सौम्यवपुर्महात्मा ॥५०॥

दृष्ट्वेदं मानुषं रूपं तव सौम्यं जनार्दन ।
इदानीमस्मि संवृत्तः सचेताः प्रकृतिं गतः ॥५१॥

सुदुर्दर्शमिदं रूपं दृष्टवानसि यन्मम ।
देवा अप्यस्य रूपस्य नित्यं दर्शनकाङ्क्षिणः ॥५२॥

नाहं वेदैर्न तपसा न दानेन न चेज्यया ।
शक्य एवंविधो द्रष्टुं दृष्टवानसि मां यथा ॥५३॥

Sanjay said:

After saying this,

Bhagvan appeared again in his gentle four armed form

and comforted Arjun.

Arjun said:

Oh Krishna,

seeing Your gentle form again,

I am calm.

Bhagvan replied:

This form of Mine is very hard to see.

Even the gods are always anxious to see it.

I cannot be seen in this form

through studying the Vedas or through suffering.

I cannot be seen through charity or in ceremonies.

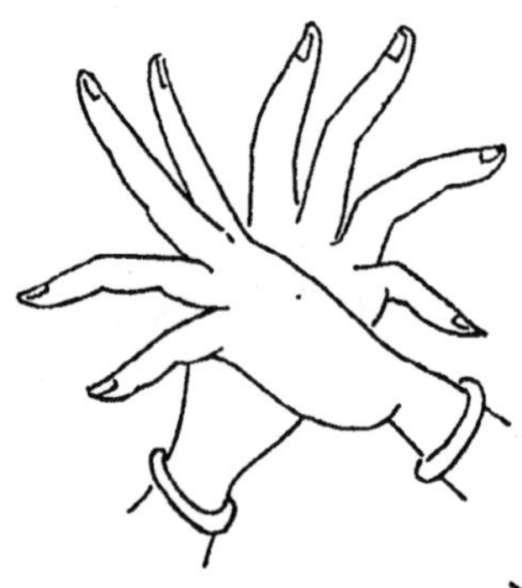

भक्त्या त्वनन्यया शक्य अहमेवंविधोऽर्जुन ।
ज्ञातुं द्रष्टुं च तत्त्वेन प्रवेष्टुं च परंतप ॥५४॥

मत्कर्मकृन्मत्परमो मद्भक्तः संगवर्जितः ।
निर्वैरः सर्वभूतेषु यः स मामेति पाण्डव ॥५५॥

But by endless love

I can be seen in this four armed form.

By endless love

I can be known.

By endless love

I can be entered into.

Oh Arjun,

whoever works for My sake alone, reaches Me.

Whoever trusts Me, loves Me,

loves nothing else,

and is full of kindness toward all living beings,

reaches Me.

श्री

द्वादशोऽध्यायः

एवं सततयुक्ता ये भक्तास्त्वां पर्युपासते ।
ये चाप्यक्षरमव्यक्तं तेषां के योगवित्तमाः ॥ १ ॥

मय्यावेश्य मनो ये मां नित्ययुक्ता उपासते ।
श्रद्धया परयोपेतास्ते मे युक्ततमा मताः ॥ २ ॥

ये त्वक्षरमनिर्देश्यमव्यक्तं पर्युपासते ।
सर्वत्रगमचिन्त्यं च कूटस्थमचलं ध्रुवम् ॥ ३ ॥

संनियम्येन्द्रियग्रामं सर्वत्र समबुद्धयः ।
ते प्राप्नुवन्ति मामेव सर्वभूतहिते रताः ॥ ४ ॥

Chapter 12

Loving God

Arjun said:

Some people who love You, have a picture of You
in their mind. Other people love You
just as a formless, nameless, endless God.
Which people are the best?

Bhagvan answered:

I think those who love and trust Me most
and always think of Me are the best.
But those who have self control and are calm
and do good to all also come to me.
Those who never stop loving God,
even without imagining what God is like,
they too come to Me.

क्लेशोऽधिकतरस्तेषामव्यक्तासक्तचेतसाम् ।
अव्यक्ता हि गतिर्दुःखं देहवद्भिरवाप्यते ॥ ५ ॥
ये तु सर्वाणि कर्माणि मयि संन्यस्य मत्पराः ।
अनन्येनैव योगेन मां ध्यायन्त उपासते ॥ ६ ॥
तेषामहं समुद्धर्ता मृत्युसंसारसागरात् ।
भवामि न चिरात्पार्थ मय्यावेशितचेतसाम् ॥ ७ ॥

मय्येव मन आधत्स्व मयि बुद्धिं निवेशय ।
निवसिष्यसि मय्येव अत ऊर्ध्वं न संशयः ॥ ८ ॥

अथ चित्तं समाधातुं न शक्नोषि मयि स्थिरम् ।
अभ्यासयोगेन ततो मामिच्छाप्तुं धनञ्जय ॥ ९ ॥
अभ्यासेऽप्यसमर्थोऽसि मत्कर्मपरमो भव ।
मदर्थमपि कर्माणि कुर्वन्सिद्धिमवाप्स्यसि ॥ १० ॥
अथैतदप्यशक्तोऽसि कर्तुं मद्योगमाश्रितः ।
सर्वकर्मफलत्यागं ततः कुरु यतात्मवान् ॥ ११ ॥

Of course, it is harder to love God
without imagining what He is like.

But I quickly rescue from birth and death
whoever loves only Me
and does everything for Me only
and worships Me all the time.

So think of Me and you will surely love Me.
If you cannot think of Me steadily, without stopping,
then you must practice.
If you cannot even practice, then do all you can
for My sake.
You will become perfect
just by doing things for My sake.
If you cannot manage even this, then just remember
not to worry about the results of what you do.

श्रेयो हि ज्ञानमभ्यासाज्ज्ञानाद्ध्यानं विशिष्यते ।
ध्यानात्कर्मफलत्यागस्त्यागाच्छान्तिरनन्तरम् ॥१२॥

अद्वेष्टा सर्वभूतानां मैत्रः करुण एव च ।
निर्ममो निरहंकारः समदुःखसुखः क्षमी ॥१३॥

संतुष्टः सततं योगी यतात्मा दृढनिश्चयः ।
मय्यर्पितमनोबुद्धिर्यो मद्भक्तः स मे प्रियः ॥१४॥

Do not plan for things to turn out
the way you want them to,
but simply do your best. Do your best
and don't think about what will happen next.

Knowledge is better than practice
and thinking steadily of God is better than knowledge.
But best of all is doing your duty for God's sake.

She who hates no one,
who is friendly, kind and unselfish
is dear to God.
She who does not worry about suffering or pain
is dear to Me.
She who does not hope for pleasures
and is forgiving and always happy
is dear to Me.

यस्मान्नोद्विजते लोको लोकान्नोद्विजते च यः ।
हर्षामर्षभयोद्वेगैर्मुक्तो यः स च मे प्रियः ॥१५॥

अनपेक्षः शुचिर्दक्ष उदासीनो गतव्यथः ।
सर्वारम्भपरित्यागी यो मद्भक्तः स मे प्रियः ॥१६॥

He whose mind is joined to God,
whose body obeys his mind,
and whose mind belongs to God,
that person is very dear to God.

He who does no harm in the world
and who loves the world is dear to Me.
He who is always calm
and who is not happy and excited one moment
but angry the next, is dear to Me.
He who is unafraid is dear to Me.

He who wants nothing,
who is pure and faithful is dear to Me.
He who understands that all he does
is really done by God,
that person is dear to Me.

यो न हृष्यति न द्वेष्टि न शोचति न काङ्क्षति ।
शुभाशुभपरित्यागी भक्तिमान्यः स मे प्रियः ॥१७॥

समः शत्रौ च मित्रे च तथा मानापमानयोः ।
शीतोष्णसुखदुःखेषु समः संगविवर्जितः ॥१८॥

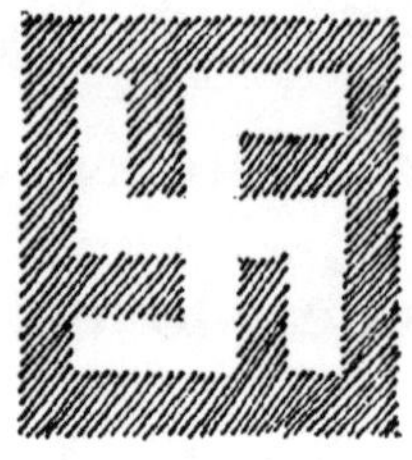

तुल्यनिन्दास्तुतिर्मौनी संतुष्टो येन केनचित् ।
अनिकेतः स्थिरमतिर्भक्तिमान्मे प्रियो नरः ॥१९॥

ये तु धर्म्यामृतमिदं यथोक्तं पर्युपासते ।
श्रद्दधाना मत्परमा भक्तास्तेऽतीव मे प्रियाः ॥२०॥

She who does not jump with joy
or hate or suffer or want things
is dear to Me.
She who gives up both good and bad,
and loves only God is dear to Me.

She who treats friends and enemies alike
is dear to Me.
She who doesn't care if she is praised or criticized,
or if she is hot or cold, or happy or unhappy,
She is dear to Me.

They who understand
and follow all these teachings of Mine
are dear to Me.
The person who loves nothing but God, only God,
is very dear to Me.

श्री

त्रयोदशोऽध्यायः

इदं शरीरं कौंतेय क्षेत्रमित्यभिधीयते ।
एतद्यो वेत्ति तं प्राहुः क्षेत्रज्ञ इति तद्विदः ॥ १ ॥

क्षेत्रज्ञं चापि मां विद्धि सर्वक्षेत्रेषु भारत ।
क्षेत्रक्षेत्रज्ञयोर्ज्ञानं यत्तज्ज्ञानं मतं मम ॥ २ ॥

तत्क्षेत्रं यच्च यादृक् च यद्विकारि यतश्च यत् ।
स च यो यत्प्रभावश्च तत्समासेन मे शृणु ॥ ३ ॥

ऋषिभिर्बहुधा गीतं छन्दोभिर्विविधैः पृथक् ।
ब्रह्मसूत्रपदैश्चैव हेतुमद्भिर्विनिश्चितैः ॥ ४ ॥

Chapter 13

The Body and The Spirit

Bhagvan said:

Oh Kunti's son,

The body is called the Kshetra, or the field.

I, God,

am called the Kshetrajna, or the Knower of the field.

I am the Self or Atman.

I am the Spirit.

Now I will tell you in a second

the truth

about the body.

महाभूतान्यहंकारो बुद्धिरव्यक्तमेव च ।
इन्द्रियाणि दशैकं च पञ्च चेन्द्रियगोचराः ॥५॥
इच्छा द्वेषः सुखं दुःखं संघातश्चेतना धृतिः ।
एतत्क्षेत्रं समासेन सविकारमुदाहृतम् ॥६॥
अमानित्वमदम्भित्वमहिंसा क्षान्तिरार्जवम् ।
आचार्योपासनं शौचं स्थैर्यमात्मविनिग्रहः ॥७॥

इन्द्रियार्थेषु वैराग्यमनहंकार एव च ।
जन्ममृत्युजराव्याधिदुःखदोषानुदर्शनम् ॥८॥

असक्तिरनभिष्वङ्गः पुत्रदारगृहादिषु ।
नित्यं च समचित्तत्वमिष्टानिष्टोपपत्तिषु ॥९॥
मयि चानन्ययोगेन भक्तिरव्यभिचारिणी ।
विविक्तदेशसेवित्वमरतिर्जनसंसदि ॥१०॥
अध्यात्मज्ञाननित्यत्वं तत्त्वज्ञानार्थदर्शनम् ।
एतज्ज्ञानमिति प्रोक्तमज्ञानं यदतोऽन्यथा ॥११॥

The body is a collection of many things.

It is made up of ether, air, fire, water, and earth.

These are called the five subtle elements.

The body is also made up of mind,

and the five senses of hearing,

touching, seeing, tasting and smelling.

Wanting, hating, happiness, unhappiness and courage

are also a part of the body.

Knowledge is many good things.

It is being honest, kind, forgiving and pure

and it is also concentrating on God.

It is not caring about anything except God.

It is not worrying.

Knowledge is seeing God everywhere.

The opposite of all these good things is ignorance.

Ignorance is the opposite of knowledge.

ज्ञेयं यत्तत्प्रवक्ष्यामि यज्ज्ञात्वाऽमृतमश्नुते ।
अनादिमत्परं ब्रह्म न सत्तन्नासदुच्यते ॥१२॥

सर्वतः पाणिपादं तत्सर्वतोऽक्षिशिरोमुखम् ।
सर्वतः श्रुतिमल्लोके सर्वमावृत्य तिष्ठति ॥१३॥

सर्वेन्द्रियगुणाभासं सर्वेन्द्रियविवर्जितम् ।
असक्तं सर्वभृच्चैव निर्गुणं गुणभोक्तृ च ॥१४॥

बहिरन्तश्च भूतानामचरं चरमेव च ।
सूक्ष्मत्वात्तदविज्ञेयं दूरस्थं चान्तिके च तत् ॥१५॥

अविभक्तं च भूतेषु विभक्तमिव च स्थितम् ।
भूतभर्तृ च तज्ज्ञेयं ग्रसिष्णु प्रभविष्णु च ॥१६॥

ज्योतिषामपि तज्ज्योतिस्तमसः परमुच्यते ।
ज्ञानं ज्ञेयं ज्ञानगम्यं हृदि सर्वस्य धिष्ठितम् ॥१७॥

Now I will tell you what you need to know

to become everlasting.

God is not Sat, real and God is not Asat, unreal.

Brahma has hands, feet, eyes, heads, faces, and ears

everywhere. Brahma is everywhere.

Brahma sees and feels everything

without eyes or hands.

Brahma is outside and inside everything

and near and far. Brahma is too great to be known.

God cannot be divided but He is everywhere.

He keeps the world, He destroys the world,

and He creates the world.

God is the light of all lights.

God is past Maya, or make believe.

God is knowing and God is knowledge.

God is in your heart.

इति क्षेत्रं तथा ज्ञानं ज्ञेयं चोक्तं समासतः ।
मद्भक्त एतद्विज्ञाय मद्भावायोपपद्यते ॥१८॥

प्रकृतिं पुरुषं चैव विद्ध्यनादी उभावपि ।
विकारांश्च गुणांश्चैव विद्धि प्रकृतिसंभवान् ॥१९॥

कार्यकारणकर्तृत्वे हेतुः प्रकृतिरुच्यते ।
पुरुषः सुखदुःखानां भोक्तृत्वे हेतुरुच्यते ॥२०॥

पुरुषः प्रकृतिस्थो हि भुंक्ते प्रकृतिजान्गुणान् ।
कारणं गुणसंगोऽस्य सदसद्योनिजन्मसु ॥२१॥

उपद्रष्टानुमंता च भर्ता भोक्ता महेश्वरः ।
परमात्मेति चाप्युक्तो देहेऽस्मिन्पुरुषः परः ॥२२॥

य एवं वेत्ति पुरुषं प्रकृतिं च गुणैः सह ।
सर्वथा वर्तमानोऽपि न स भूयोऽभिजायते ॥२३॥

By understanding all this,
you can be mixed with God.
Everything in the world
is a combination
of matter and spirit.
Matter makes the body.
Spirit makes the body feel things.
Everything that is born in the world
is created
by joining matter and spirit together.
But matter and spirit have no beginning.

The spirit cannot be described.
Though it lives in the body, it cannot act.
It is always pure.
It is endless as the sun and the sky.

ध्यानेनात्मनि पश्यंति केचिदात्मानमात्मना ।
अन्ये सांख्येन योगेन कर्मयोगेन चापरे ॥२४॥
अन्ये त्वेवमजानंतः श्रुत्वान्येभ्य उपासते ।
तेऽपि चातितरंत्येव मृत्युं श्रुतिपरायणाः ॥२५॥
यावत्संजायते किंचित्सत्त्वं स्थावरजंगमम् ।
क्षेत्रक्षेत्रज्ञसंयोगात्तद्विद्धि भरतर्षभ ॥२६॥

समं सर्वेषु भूतेषु तिष्ठन्तं परमेश्वरम् ।
विनश्यत्स्वविनश्यन्तं यः पश्यति स पश्यति ॥२७॥

समं पश्यन्हि सर्वत्र समवस्थितमीश्वरम् ।
न हिनस्त्यात्मनाऽऽत्मानं ततो याति परां गतिम् ॥२८॥
प्रकृत्यैव च कर्माणि क्रियमाणानि सर्वशः ।
यः पश्यति तथाऽऽत्मानमकर्तारं स पश्यति ॥२९॥
यदा भूतपृथग्भावमेकस्थमनुपश्यति ।
तत एव च विस्तारं ब्रह्म संपद्यते तदा ॥३०॥

The greatest spirit is the soul.
It is God.

Some people find the soul in their own heart
by thinking of God,
by understanding God,
or by working for God's sake.

Some people find God by hearing about Him
from others.

She who sees the soul, the Lord, as everlasting
really sees the truth.

When you see that everything is in God
and comes from God,
then you reach God.

अनादित्वान्निर्गुणत्वात्परमात्माऽयमव्ययः ।
शरीरस्थोऽपि कौन्तेय न करोति न लिप्यते ॥३१॥

यथा सर्वगतं सौक्ष्म्यादाकाशं नोपलिप्यते ।
सर्वत्रावस्थितो देहे तथात्मा नोपलिप्यते ॥३२॥

यथा प्रकाशयत्येकः कृत्स्नं लोकमिमं रविः ।
क्षेत्रं क्षेत्री तथा कृत्स्नं प्रकाशयति भारत ॥३३॥

क्षेत्रक्षेत्रज्ञयोरेवमन्तरं ज्ञानचक्षुषा ।
भूतप्रकृतिमोक्षं च ये विदुर्यान्ति ते परम् ॥३४॥

Arjun,
like the sun lights the whole world,
so one great spirit, the soul,
called Atman
lights the whole body.

Wise people can tell
the difference between the body and the spirit.
They understand
how to free the spirit from the body.
These wise people come straight to God.

श्री

चतुर्दशोऽध्यायः

परं भूयः प्रवक्ष्यामि ज्ञानानां ज्ञानमुत्तमम् ।
यज्ज्ञात्वा मुनयः सर्वे परां सिद्धिमितो गताः ॥ १ ॥

इदं ज्ञानमुपाश्रित्य मम साधर्म्यमागताः ।
सर्गेऽपि नोपजायन्ते प्रलये न व्यथन्ति च ॥ २ ॥

मम योनिर्महद्ब्रह्म तस्मिन्गर्भं दधाम्यहम् ।
संभवः सर्वभूतानां ततो भवति भारत ॥ ३ ॥

सर्वयोनिषु कौन्तेय मूर्तयः संभवन्ति याः ।
तासां ब्रह्म महद्योनिरहं बीजप्रदः पिता ॥ ४ ॥

Chapter 14

Sattva, Rajas, and Tamas

Bhagvan said:

Arjun,

I will share the greatest truth with you again.

Knowing this, people become part of me

and do not have to be born again

when the world is created.

Knowing the truth, people do not have to suffer

when the world is destroyed.

Everything is born

when the body and the spirit join together.

The body is the Mother

and I, God, am the Father.

सत्त्वं रजस्तम इति गुणाः प्रकृतिसंभवाः ।
निबध्नन्ति महाबाहो देहे देहिनमव्ययम् ॥ ५ ॥

तत्र सत्त्वं निर्मलत्वात्प्रकाशकमनामयम् ।
सुखसंगेन बध्नाति ज्ञानसंगेन चानघ ॥ ६ ॥

रजो रागात्मकं विद्धि तृष्णासंगसमुद्भवम् ।
तन्निबध्नाति कौन्तेय कर्मसंगेन देहिनम् ॥ ७ ॥

तमस्त्वज्ञानजं विद्धि मोहनं सर्वदेहिनाम् ।
प्रमादालस्यनिद्राभिस्तन्निबध्नाति भारत ॥ ८ ॥

सत्त्वं सुखे सञ्जयति रजः कर्मणि भारत ।
ज्ञानमावृत्य तु तमः प्रमादे सञ्जयत्युत ॥ ९ ॥

रजस्तमश्चाभिभूय सत्त्वं भवति भारत ।
रजः सत्त्वं तमश्चैव तमः सत्त्वं रजस्तथा ॥ १० ॥

The body has three parts
or three gunas called Sattva, Rajas, and Tamas.
These three tie the soul to the body.
We are made up of Sattva, Rajas, and Tamas.

Sattva is good.
It is clean and shining.
It is healthy and has no faults.
Sattva is happy and calm.

Rajas is not good.
It is greedy and active
and causes strong feelings.

Tamas is bad because it comes from ignorance.
It is full of faults and mistakes.
Tamas is lazy.

सर्वद्वारेषु देहेऽस्मिन् प्रकाश उपजायते ।
ज्ञानं यदा तदा विद्याद्विवृद्धं सत्त्वमित्युत ॥११॥

लोभः प्रवृत्तिरारम्भः कर्मणामशमः स्पृहा ।
रजस्येतानि जायन्ते विवृद्धे भरतर्षभ ॥१२॥

अप्रकाशोऽप्रवृत्तिश्च प्रमादो मोह एव च ।
तमस्येतानि जायन्ते विवृद्धे कुरुनन्दन ॥१३॥

यदा सत्त्वे प्रवृद्धे तु प्रलयं याति देहभृत् ।
तदोत्तमविदां लोकानमलान्प्रतिपद्यते ॥१४॥

रजसि प्रलयं गत्वा कर्मसंगिषु जायते ।
तथा प्रलीनस्तमसि मूढयोनिषु जायते ॥१५॥

These three things are mixed up in us,
but the strongest part makes us good or bad.
When Sattva is strongest, we are wise.
When Rajas is strongest, we are greedy
and we cannot keep calm or still.
When Tamas is strongest,
we are lazy, foolish and covered by darkness.

If when we die,
we are mostly Sattva,
our spirit gets born again
in the world of the wise and the pure.
If we are mostly Rajas,
our spirit gets born again on earth.
If we are mostly Tamas,
our spirit gets born
in the body of a dumb, ignorant being.

कर्मणः सुकृतस्याहुः सात्त्विकं निर्मलं फलम् ।
रजसस्तु फलं दुःखमज्ञानं तमसः फलम् ॥१६॥

सत्त्वात्सञ्जायते ज्ञानं रजसो लोभ एव च ।
प्रमादमोहौ तमसो भवतोऽज्ञानमेव च ॥१७॥

ऊर्ध्वं गच्छन्ति सत्त्वस्था मध्ये तिष्ठन्ति राजसाः ।
जघन्यगुणवृत्तिस्था अधो गच्छन्ति तामसाः ॥१८॥

नान्यं गुणेभ्यः कर्तारं यदा द्रष्टानुपश्यति ।
गुणेभ्यश्च परं वेत्ति मद्भावं सोऽधिगच्छति ॥१९॥

गुणानेतानतीत्य त्रीन् देही देहसमुद्भवान् ।
जन्ममृत्युजरादुःखैर्विमुक्तोऽमृतमश्नुते ॥२०॥

The fruit, or the result, of Sattva
is pure goodness.
The fruit of Rajas is sorrow.
The fruit of Tamas is ignorance.

From Sattva comes wisdom.
From Rajas comes greed.
From Tamas come mistakes and ignorance.

But if you understand
that God is past Sattva, Rajas, and Tamas,
your spirit will be freed from the body.
It will not have to be born again
and you will go straight to God.

कैर्लिङ्गैस्त्रीन् गुणानेतानतीतो भवति प्रभो ।
किमाचारः कथं चैतांस्त्रीन्गुणानतिवर्तते ॥२१॥

प्रकाशं च प्रवृत्तिं च मोहमेव च पाण्डव ।
न द्वेष्टि संप्रवृत्तानि न निवृत्तानि काङ्क्षति ॥२२॥

उदासीनवदासीनो गुणैर्यो न विचाल्यते ।
गुणा वर्तन्त इत्येव योऽवतिष्ठति नेङ्गते ॥२३॥

समदुःखसुखः स्वस्थः समलोष्टाश्मकाञ्चनः ।
तुल्यप्रियाप्रियो धीरस्तुल्यनिन्दात्मसंस्तुतिः ॥२४॥

मानापमानयोस्तुल्यस्तुल्यो मित्रारिपक्षयोः ।
सर्वारम्भपरित्यागी गुणातीतः स उच्यते ॥२५॥

Then Arjun asked:
How can I recognize a person
whose spirit is freed from her body?
How can we go past the three gunas
which bind the soul?

Bhagvan answered:
The person who is free
does not care what happens to her body.
Whoever feels the same
about pleasant and unpleasant things
has crossed beyond Sattva, Rajas, and Tamas.
Whoever likes stone as much as gold is wise.
Whoever treats friends and enemies the same way,
and does her duty,
not caring if she is praised or scolded, is free.
Such a person has gone past the three gunas.

मां च योऽव्यभिचारेण भक्तियोगेन सेवते ।
स गुणान्समतीत्यैतान् ब्रह्मभूयाय कल्पते ॥२६॥

ब्रह्मणो हि प्रतिष्ठाहममृतस्याव्ययस्य च ।
शाश्वतस्य च धर्मस्य सुखस्यैकान्तिकस्य च ॥२७॥

She who always worships God faithfully

crosses past the world,

and becomes a part of God.

I am God.

I am Brahma's home.

I am everlasting and unchanging.

I am unending goodness

and unending joy.

श्री

पञ्चदशोऽध्यायः

उर्ध्वमूलमधःशाखमश्वत्थं प्राहुरव्ययम् ।
छन्दांसि यस्य पर्णानि यस्तं वेद स वेदवित् ॥ १ ॥

अधश्चोर्ध्वं प्रसृतास्तस्य शाखा
गुणप्रवृद्धा विषयप्रवालाः ।
अधश्च मूलान्यनुसंततानि
कर्मानुबन्धीनि मनुष्यलोके ॥ २ ॥

Chapter 15

The Excellent Spirit

Bhagvan said:

The Tree of Life,

The Peepal Tree, is like the world.

Its root is God.

Its stem is Brahma, the Creator.

Its leaves are the holy books

known as the Vedas.

Like the branches of the tree

which go both up and down,

the deeds of man

can lift him up or lower him down.

न रूपमस्येह तथोपलभ्यते
नान्तो न चादिर्न च संप्रतिष्ठा ।
अश्वत्थमेनं सुविरूढमूल-
मसङ्गशस्त्रेण दृढेन छित्त्वा ॥ ३ ॥

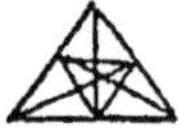

ततः पदं तत्परिमार्गितव्यं
यस्मिन्गता न निवर्तन्ति भूयः ।
तमेव चाद्यं पुरुषं प्रपद्ये
यतः प्रवृत्तिः प्रसृता पुराणी ॥ ४ ॥

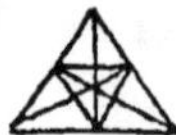

निर्मानमोहा जितसङ्गदोषा
अध्यात्मनित्या विनिवृत्तकामाः ।
द्वन्द्वैर्विमुक्ताः सुखदुःखसंज्ञै-
र्गच्छन्त्यमूढाः पदमव्ययं तत् ॥ ५ ॥

न तद्भासयते सूर्यो न शशाङ्को न पावकः ।
यद्गत्वा न निवर्तन्ते तद्धाम परमं मम ॥ ६ ॥

But to reach the inside spirit of the tree,
the seed from which it was born,
we have to cut the tree down.

And to reach your spirit inside your heart,
you have to cut yourself off from life.
Cutting yourself off from life
means not caring about anything except God.
The whole world was started by God.

Only wise people can care about God alone
and get mixed with Him.
Wise people are not proud
and do not keep on wanting things.
They do not keep changing
from happiness to unhappiness.

ममैवांशो जीवलोके जीवभूतः सनातनः ।
मनःषष्ठानीन्द्रियाणि प्रकृतिस्थानि कर्षति ॥७॥

शरीरं यदवाप्नोति यच्चाप्युत्क्रामतीश्वरः ।
गृहीत्वैतानि संयाति वायुर्गन्धानिवाशयात् ॥८॥

श्रोत्रं चक्षुः स्पर्शनं च रसनं घ्राणमेव च ।
अधिष्ठाय मनश्चायं विषयानुपसेवते ॥९॥

उत्क्रामन्तं स्थितं वापि भुञ्जानं वा गुणान्वितम् ।
विमूढा नानुपश्यन्ति पश्यन्ति ज्ञानचक्षुषः ॥१०॥

You should know that My spirit is your soul.
Your soul is the spirit of God in you.
It pulls the mind and the five senses
of touching, hearing, seeing,
smelling and tasting to itself.
Your soul can blow away from your mind and body
and find a mind and body to live in.

Just as the smell of a flower
is blown by the wind,
the spirit is blown from the body.

Foolish people cannot understand
that the soul sometimes lives in the body
and sometimes leaves it.
Only people who have the eye of wisdom know this.

यतन्तो योगिनश्चैनं पश्यन्त्यात्मन्यवस्थितम् ।
यतन्तोऽप्यकृतात्मानो नैनं पश्यन्त्यचेतसः ॥११॥
यदादित्यगतं तेजो जगद्भासयतेऽखिलम् ।
यच्चन्द्रमसि यच्चाग्नौ तत्तेजो विद्धि मामकम् ॥१२॥
गामाविश्य च भूतानि धारयाम्यहमोजसा ।
पुष्णामि चौषधीः सर्वाः सोमो भूत्वा रसात्मकः ॥१३॥
अहं वैश्वानरो भूत्वा प्राणिनां देहमाश्रितः ।
प्राणापानसमायुक्तः पचाम्यन्नं चतुर्विधम् ॥१४॥

सर्वस्य चाहं हृदि संनिविष्टो
मत्तः स्मृतिर्ज्ञानमपोहनं च ।
वेदैश्च सर्वैरहमेव वेद्यो
वेदान्तकृद्वेदविदेव चाहम् ॥१५॥
द्वाविमौ पुरुषौ लोके क्षरश्चाक्षर एव च ।
क्षरः सर्वाणि भूतानि कूटस्थोऽक्षर उच्यते ॥१६॥
उत्तमः पुरुषस्त्वन्यः परमात्मेत्युदाहृतः ।
यो लोकत्रयमाविश्य बिभर्त्यव्यय ईश्वरः ॥१७॥

The foolish cannot know God.

The light in the sun which lights the whole world,
and the light in the moon,
and the light in the fire
is My light.

And I am in everyone's heart.
But only special people can find me there.
I am everyone's memory,
their wisdom and their thinking.

In this world there are two kinds of things,
unreal, make believe things that change,
and real things that are real forever.
The soul, the spirit of God in you,
is real forever.

यस्मात्क्षरमतीतोऽहमक्षरादपि चोत्तमः ।
अतोऽस्मि लोके वेदे च प्रथितः पुरुषोत्तमः ॥१८॥

यो मामेवमसंमूढो जानाति पुरुषोत्तमम् ।
स सर्वविद्भजति मां सर्वभावेन भारत ॥१९॥

इति गुह्यतमं शास्त्रमिदमुक्तं मयाऽनघ ।
एतद्बुद्ध्वा बुद्धिमान् स्यात्कृतकृत्यश्च भारत ॥२०॥

I, God, am past make believe.
I am beyond the unreal.
This is why I am called the Excellent Spirit.

Oh Arjun,
wise persons who understand
that I am the Excellent Spirit
worship Me with all their heart.

Oh Arjun,
you are without sin.
This is why I have explained My best secrets
to you.

Understanding these secrets,
people can become wise
and the light of truth will shine on them.

श्री

षोडशोऽध्यायः

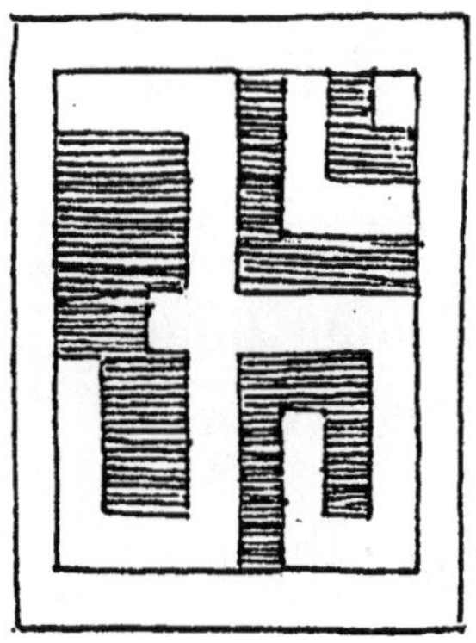

अभयं सत्त्वसंशुद्धिर्ज्ञानयोगव्यवस्थितिः ।
दानं दमश्च यज्ञश्च स्वाध्यायस्तप आर्जवम् ॥ १ ॥

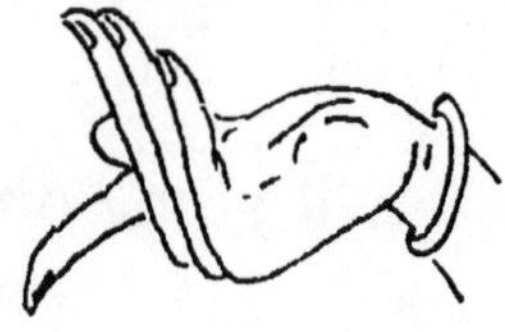

Chapter 16

Good and Evil

Bhagvan said:

Goodness is many things.

Goodness is being brave and pure

and thinking of your soul.

Your soul is God inside you.

Goodness is helping others.

It is self control and worshipping God

and having pujas

and studying the Vedas and other holy books.

It is calling out God's names and glories

and suffering for your beliefs.

Goodness is being straight and strong

in body and mind.

अहिंसा सत्यमक्रोधस्त्यागः शान्तिरपैशुनम् ।
दया भूतेष्वलोलुप्त्वं मार्दवं ह्रीरचापलम् ॥ २ ॥

तेजः क्षमा धृतिः शौचमद्रोहो नातिमानिता ।
भवन्ति संपदं दैवीमभिजातस्य भारत ॥ ३ ॥

Peacefulness, truthfulness and kindness are good.
So is not being angry, even if you have a reason.

Goodness is realizing God does things through you,
that you do not do them by yourself.

Goodness is not wanting,
being kind to all
and not caring about the pleasures of your body.
Goodness is gentleness
and being ashamed of your mistakes
and not being lazy.

Forgiveness, strength,
not being mean and not being proud
are goodness.
These are the signs of someone who is good.

दम्भो दर्पोऽभिमानश्च क्रोधः पारुष्यमेव च ।
अज्ञानं चाभिजातस्य पार्थ संपदमासुरीम् ॥ ४ ॥

दैवी संपद्विमोक्षाय निबन्धायासुरी मता ।
मा शुचः संपदं दैवीमभिजातोऽसि पाण्डव ॥ ५ ॥

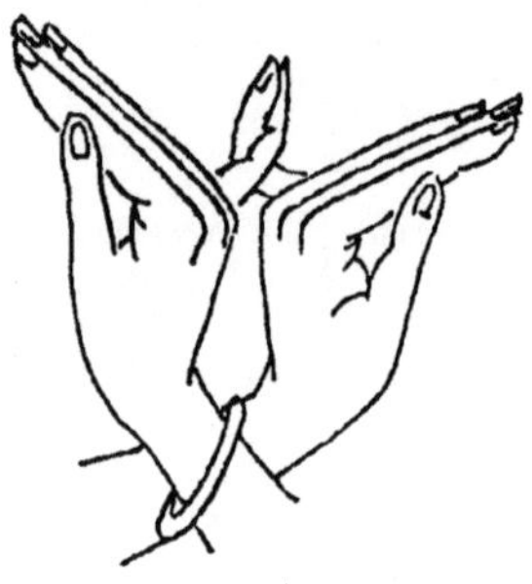

द्वौ भूतसर्गौ लोकेऽस्मिन्दैव आसुर एव च ।
दैवो विस्तरशः प्रोक्त आसुरं पार्थ मे शृणु ॥ ६ ॥

प्रवृत्तिं च निवृत्तिं च जना न विदुरासुराः ।
न शौचं नापि चाचारो न सत्यं तेषु विद्यते ॥ ७ ॥

But those who are dishonest, rude, angry,
unkind and ignorant, are bad.
These are evil, bad things.

Goodness leads to God and freedom.
Evil takes you away from God.
But do not worry, Arjun,
for you were born with goodness.

Oh Arjun, in this world there are two kinds of people,
good and evil.
I have just told you about the good kind.
Now hear about the evil kind.

People who are evil
do not know what is right or wrong.

So they cannot be pure, or behave well or be truthful.

असत्यमप्रतिष्ठं ते जगदाहुरनीश्वरम् ।
अपरस्परसंभूतं किमन्यत्कामहैतुकम् ॥८॥

श्री

एतां दृष्टिमवष्टभ्य नष्टात्मानोऽल्पबुद्धयः ।
प्रभवन्त्युग्रकर्माणः क्षयाय जगतोऽहिताः ॥९॥

काममाश्रित्य दुष्पूरं दम्भमानमदान्विताः ।
मोहाद् गृहीत्वाऽसद्ग्राहान्प्रवर्तन्तेऽशुचिव्रताः ॥१०॥

Bad people say:
"The world has no reason.
The world is a lie and there is no God."
Bad people also say:
"It is men and women
who have children and make the world,
not God."

These people who do not understand are cruel.
They are born to ruin things.

They are dishonest, proud, rude, and foolish.

The fools keep worrying and worrying.
They only care about their body.
They make wrong decisions.

चिन्तामपरिमेयां च प्रलयान्तामुपाश्रिताः ।
कामोपभोगपरमा एतावदिति निश्चिताः ॥११॥
आशापाशशतैर्बद्धाः कामक्रोधपरायणाः ।
ईहन्ते कामभोगार्थमन्यायेनार्थसंचयान् ॥१२॥

इदमद्य मया लब्धमिमं प्राप्स्ये मनोरथम् ।
इदमस्तीदमपि मे भविष्यति पुनर्धनम् ॥१३॥
असौ मया हतः शत्रुर्हनिष्ये चापरानपि ।
ईश्वरोऽहमहं भोगी सिद्धोऽहं बलवान्सुखी ॥१४॥

आढ्योऽभिजनवानस्मि कोऽन्योऽस्ति सदृशो मया ।
यक्ष्ये दास्यामि मोदिष्य इत्यज्ञानविमोहिताः ॥१५॥
अनेकचित्तविभ्रान्ता मोहजालसमावृताः ।
प्रसक्ताः कामभोगेषु पतन्ति नरकेऽशुचौ ॥१६॥

आत्मसंभाविताः स्तब्धा धनमानमदान्विताः ।
यजन्ते नामयज्ञैस्ते दम्भेनाविधिपूर्वकम् ॥१७॥
अहंकारं बलं दर्पं कामं क्रोधं च संश्रिताः ।
मामात्मपरदेहेषु प्रद्विषन्तोऽभ्यसूयकाः ॥१८॥

Fools keep wanting to have fun and more fun.
They get angry.
They try to make more and more money to have fun.
This is all they think about.
This and about how important and perfect they are.
They say to themselves:

"I am rich and important. No one is like me.
I am happy. I shall have lots of fun."
But these fools are stupid.
They pretend to worship God
but their worship is a lie.

Such fools are selfish and cruel
and they hate the God that lives in their heart
and lives in the hearts of others too.

तानहं द्विषतः क्रूरान् संसारेषु नराधमान् ।
क्षिपाम्यजस्रमशुभानासुरीष्वेव योनिषु ॥१९॥
आसुरी योनिमापन्ना मूढा जन्मनि जन्मनि ।
मामप्राप्यैव कौन्तेय ततो यान्त्यधमां गतिम् ॥२०॥
त्रिविधं नरकस्येदं द्वारं नाशनमात्मनः ।
कामः क्रोधस्तथा लोभस्तस्मादेतत्त्रयं त्यजेत् ॥२१॥

एतैर्विमुक्तः कौन्तेय तमोद्वारैस्त्रिभिर्नरः ।
आचरत्यात्मनः श्रेयस्ततो याति परां गतिम् ॥२२॥
यः शास्त्रविधिमुत्सृज्य वर्तते कामकारतः ।
न स सिद्धिमवाप्नोति न सुखं न परां गतिम् ॥२३॥
तस्माच्छास्त्रं प्रमाणं ते कार्याकार्यव्यवस्थितौ ।
ज्ञात्वा शास्त्रविधानोक्तं कर्म कर्तुमिहार्हसि ॥२४॥

And so these people are born in foolish bodies
again and again.

Oh Arjun,
three gates lead to hell.
They are desire, anger and greed.

But the person who is good and unselfish
always does what is written in the holy books.
He finds out from these books
what is right and what is wrong.

Now you know.
You know that you should do
what the holy books say
is right and good.

श्री

सप्तदशोऽध्यायः

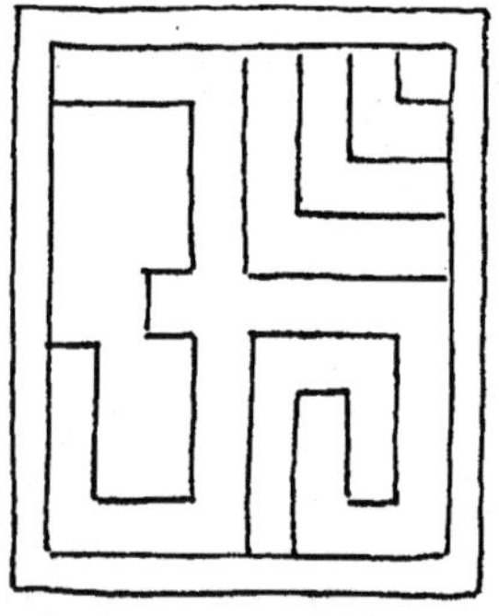

ये शास्त्रविधिमुत्सृज्य यजन्ते श्रद्धयान्विताः ।
तेषां निष्ठा तु का कृष्ण सत्त्वमाहो रजस्तमः ॥ १ ॥

त्रिविधा भवति श्रद्धा देहिनां सा स्वभावजा ।
सात्त्विकी राजसी चैव तामसी चेति तां शृणु ॥ २ ॥

Chapter 17

Three Kinds of Faith

Arjun said:

Some people have faith.

They love and trust God

but they do not always worship

the way the holy books tell them to.

Oh Lord, what kind of people are they?

Bhagvan said:

Each person loves God his own way.

He loves God according to his nature.

Loving and trusting God is everything.

Faith in God is everything.

सत्त्वानुरूपा सर्वस्य श्रद्धा भवति भारत ।
श्रद्धामयोऽयं पुरुषो यो यच्छ्रद्धः स एव सः ॥ ३ ॥
यजन्ते सात्त्विका देवान्यक्षरक्षांसि राजसाः ।
प्रेतान्भूतगणांश्चान्ये यजन्ते तामसा जनाः ॥ ४ ॥
अशास्त्रविहितं घोरं तप्यन्ते ये तपो जनाः ।
दम्भाहंकारसंयुक्ताः कामरागबलान्विताः ॥ ५ ॥

कर्षयन्तः शरीरस्थं भूतग्राममचेतसः ।
मां चैवान्तःशरीरस्थं तान्विद्ध्यासुरनिश्चयान् ॥ ६ ॥

आहारस्त्वपि सर्वस्य त्रिविधो भवति प्रियः ।
यज्ञस्तपस्तथा दानं तेषां भेदमिमं शृणु ॥ ७ ॥
आयुः सत्त्वबलारोग्यसुखप्रीतिविवर्धनाः ।
रस्याः स्निग्धाः स्थिरा हृद्या आहाराः सात्त्विकप्रियाः ॥ ८ ॥
कट्वम्ललवणात्युष्णतीक्ष्णरूक्षविदाहिनः ।
आहारा राजसस्येष्टा दुःखशोकामयप्रदाः ॥ ९ ॥

There are three kinds of faith
just like there are three kinds of food:
sweet, salty and bitter.

The best kind of faith is like sweet food.
It is the faith of people who do their duty.
They love and worship God.
They do their very best,
and they do not think of
how things will turn out.

The second kind of faith is like salty food.
It is worshipping God
and praying for a reward,
instead of praying
just because you love God.

यातयामं गतरसं पूति पर्युषितं च यत् ।
उच्छिष्टमपि चामेध्यं भोजनं तामसप्रियम् ॥१०॥
अफलाकाङ्क्षिभिर्यज्ञो विधिदृष्टो य इज्यते ।
यष्टव्यमेवेति मनः समाधाय स सात्त्विकः ॥११॥
अभिसंधाय तु फलं दम्भार्थमपि चैव यत् ।
इज्यते भरतश्रेष्ठ तं यज्ञं विद्धि राजसम् ॥१२॥

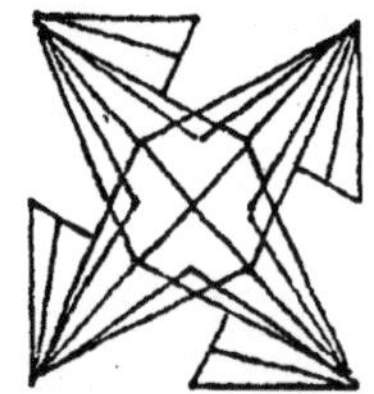

विधिहीनमसृष्टान्नं मंत्रहीनमदक्षिणाम् ।
श्रद्धाविरहितं यज्ञं तामसं परिचक्षते ॥१३॥

देवद्विजगुरुप्राज्ञपूजनं शौचमार्जवम् ।
ब्रह्मचर्यमहिंसा च शारीरं तप उच्यते ॥१४॥
अनुद्वेगकरं वाक्यं सत्यं प्रियहितं च यत् ।
स्वाध्यायाभ्यसनं चैव वाङ्मयं तप उच्यते ॥१५॥
मनःप्रसादः सौम्यत्वं मौनमात्मविनिग्रहः ।
भावसंशुद्धिरित्येतत्तपो मानसमुच्यते ॥१६॥

The third kind of faith is not real.
It is like bitter, rotten food.
It is pretending.
False spoiled faith is worshipping God just for show,
without real prayers and without love.

The best kind of worship, the sweet kind,
is having a pure body, pure speech and a pure mind.

Having a pure body
means being peaceful and having self control.
Having pure speech means
saying only kind and beautiful things
and studying holy prayers and stories.
Having a pure mind means
being cheerful and calm
and thinking of God.

श्रद्धया परया तप्तं तपस्तत् त्रिविधं नरैः ।
अफलाकाङ्क्षिभिर्युक्तैः सात्त्विकं परिचक्षते ॥१७॥

सत्कारमानपूजार्थं तपो दम्भेन चैव यत् ।
क्रियते तदिह प्रोक्तं राजसं चलमध्रुवम् ॥१८॥

मूढग्राहेणात्मनो यत्पीडया क्रियते तपः ।
परस्योत्सादनार्थं वा तत्तामसमुदाहृतम् ॥१९॥

Some people try to understand God

by making their bodies suffer

so they can realize that the body doesn't matter.

This is called tup or penance.

There are three kinds of penance.

Penance done just for God's sake is sweet.

It is like Sattva.

Penance which is done just to show off

has no value.

It is like Rajas

or like food which is salty or sour.

Penance which is done foolishly to hurt the body

or to hurt others is harmful.

It is impure like Tamas.

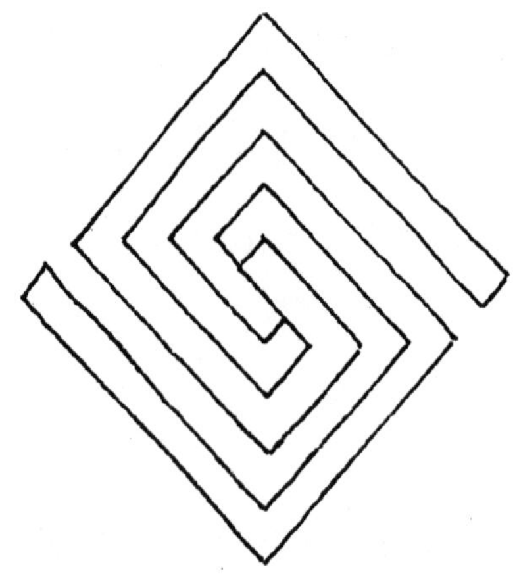

दातव्यमिति यद्दानं दीयतेऽनुपकारिणे ।
देशे काले च पात्रे च तद्दानं सात्त्विकं स्मृतम् ॥२०॥

यत्तु प्रत्युपकारार्थं फलमुद्दिश्य वा पुनः ।
दीयते च परिक्लिष्टं तद्दानं राजसं स्मृतम् ॥२१॥

अदेशकाले यद्दानमपात्रेभ्यश्च दीयते ।
असत्कृतमवज्ञातं तत्तामसमुदाहृतम् ॥२२॥

There are also three kinds of gifts.

Gifts which are Sattva are given with care

and out of duty,

not because you want something back in return.

Gifts to be Sattva should be given with love,

at the right time, in the right place,

and to the right persons.

Gifts which are given to get something back in return

are Rajas.

They are given with a grudge, not freely.

The worst kind of gifts are Tamas.

They are given at the wrong time, in the wrong place

and to wrong persons.

Tamas gifts are made

without respect in an insulting way.

ॐ तत्सदिति निर्देशो ब्रह्मणस्त्रिविधः स्मृतः ।
ब्राह्मणास्तेन वेदाश्च यज्ञाश्च विहिताः पुरा ॥२३॥

तस्मादोमित्युदाहृत्य यज्ञदानतपःक्रियाः ।
प्रवर्तन्ते विधानोक्ताः सततं ब्रह्मवादिनाम् ॥२४॥

तदित्यनभिसंधाय फलं यज्ञतपःक्रियाः ।
दानक्रियाश्च विविधाः क्रियन्ते मोक्षकाङ्क्षिभिः ॥२५॥

सद्भावे साधुभावे च सदित्येतत्प्रयुज्यते ।
प्रशस्ते कर्मणि तथा सच्छब्दः पार्थ युज्यते ।२६॥

यज्ञे तपसि दाने च स्थितिः सदिति चोच्यते ।
कर्म चैव तदर्थीयं सदित्येवाभिधीयते ॥२७॥

अश्रद्धया हुतं दत्तं तपस्तप्तं कृतं च यत् ।
असदित्युच्यते पार्थ न च तत्प्रेत्य नो इह ॥२८॥

Then the Lord said:

Listen to the words Om Tat Sat.

They are holy words.

Om means God.

Tat means everything in the world is God's.

Sat means truth and goodness.

Those who want to reach God say Om Tat Sat.

These three words explain God.

Oh Arjun,

worshipping God just for show and not for love

is not real.

Worshipping God without faith is false.

It doesn't count at all.

It is Asat which means not real.

It is nothing, nothing at all.

श्री

अथाष्टादशोऽध्यायः

संन्यासस्य महाबाहो तत्त्वमिच्छामि वेदितुम् ।
त्यागस्य च हृषीकेश पृथक्केशिनिषूदन ॥ १ ॥

काम्यानां कर्मणां न्यासं संन्यासं कवयो विदुः ।
सर्वकर्मफलत्यागं प्राहुस्त्यागं विचक्षणाः ॥ २ ॥

त्याज्यं दोषवदित्येके कर्म प्राहुर्मनीषिणः ।
यज्ञदानतपःकर्म न त्याज्यमिति चापरे ॥ ३ ॥

Chapter 18

Giving Yourself Up To God

Arjun said:

Oh Mighty God,

I want to know

what giving everything up for You means.

Bhagvan answered:

Some people believe

it means giving up doing things altogether.

They think

you should give up action completely

because action is bad.

निश्चयं शृणु मे तत्र त्यागे भरतसत्तम ।
त्यागो हि पुरुषव्याघ्र त्रिविधः संप्रकीर्तितः ॥ ४ ॥

यज्ञदानतपःकर्म न त्याज्यं कार्यमेव तत् ।
यज्ञो दानं तपश्चैव पावनानि मनीषिणाम् ॥ ५ ॥

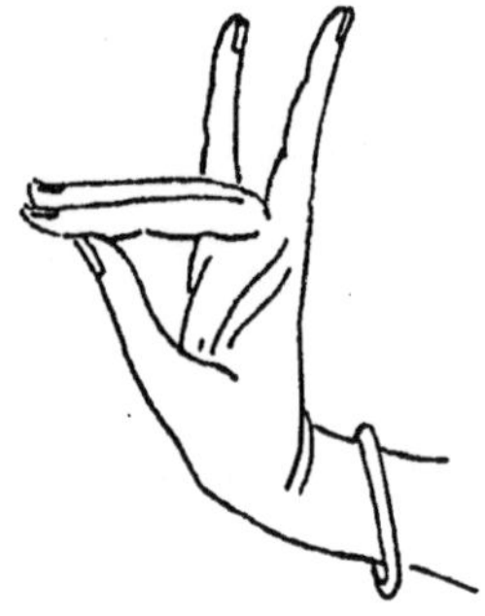

एतान्यपि तु कर्माणि सङ्गं त्यक्त्वा फलानिच ।
कर्तव्यानीति मे पार्थ निश्चितं मतमुत्तमम् ॥ ६ ॥

नियतस्य तु संन्यासः कर्मणो नोपपद्यते ।
मोहात्तस्य परित्यागस्तामसः परिकीर्तितः ॥ ७ ॥

But other wise men think it means
doing good things for God.
They believe
you should do your duty without attachment.
Without attachment is without thinking
or worrying about how everything will turn out.

Now I will tell you what I, God, believe.

Oh Arjun,
listen.
You should not give up helping others.
You should not give up religious ceremonies like pujas
and only sit doing nothing.
You should not give up things
which the holy books say are good.
Those things make you pure and good.

दुःखमित्येव यत्कर्म कायक्लेशभयात्त्यजेत् ।
स कृत्वा राजसं त्यागं नैव त्यागफलं लभेत् ॥८॥

कार्यमित्येव यत्कर्म नियतं क्रियतेऽर्जुन ।
सङ्गं त्यक्त्वा फलं चैव स त्यागः सात्त्विको मतः ।९॥

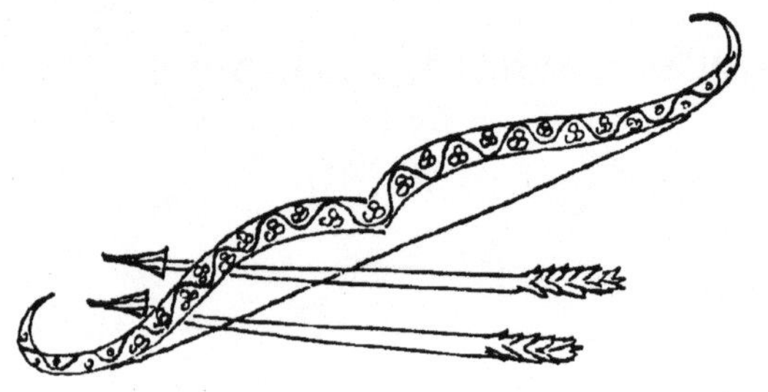

न द्वेष्ट्यकुशलं कर्म कुशले नानुषज्जते ।
त्यागी सत्त्वसमाविष्टो मेधावी छिन्नसंशयः ॥१०॥

न हि देहभृता शक्यं त्यक्तुं कर्माण्यशेषतः ।
यस्तु कर्मफलत्यागी स त्यागीत्यभिधीयते ॥११॥

You should not give up your duty
just because it is hard.
That is wrong.

You should do your duty and not think
about how the things you do will turn out.
Just do your best and do not worry about anything.
This is called
giving up the fruit of your action.
This is very good.
Giving up the fruit of your action
will make you free and happy.
Giving up the fruit of your action
is giving yourself up to God.

Wise people do their duty
without caring whether it is enjoyable or disagreeable.

अनिष्टमिष्टं मिश्रं च त्रिविधं कर्मणः फलम् ।
भवत्यत्यागिनां प्रेत्य न तु संन्यासिनां क्वचित् ॥१२॥
पञ्चैतानि महाबाहो कारणानि निबोध मे ।
सांख्ये कृतान्ते प्रोक्तानि सिद्धये सर्वकर्मणाम् ॥१३॥
अधिष्ठानं तथा कर्ता करणं च पृथग्विधम् ।
विविधाश्च पृथक्चेष्टा दैवं चैवात्र पञ्चमम् ॥१४॥

शरीरवाङ्मनोभिर्यत्कर्म प्रारभते नरः ।
न्याय्यं वा विपरीतं वा पञ्चैते तस्य हेतवः ॥१५॥

तत्रैवं सति कर्तारमात्मानं केवलं तु यः ।
पश्यत्यकृतबुद्धित्वान्न स पश्यति दुर्मतिः ॥१६॥
यस्य नाहंकृतो भावो बुद्धिर्यस्य न लिप्यते ।
हत्वापि स इमाँल्लोकान्न हन्ति न निबध्यते ॥१७॥
ज्ञानं ज्ञेयं परिज्ञाता त्रिविधा कर्मचोदना ।
करणं कर्म कर्तेति त्रिविधः कर्मसंग्रहः ॥१८॥

The things you do may turn out to be good or bad.

But if you have done your best

and do not care about how your actions turn out,

you will be happy and free.

You will be like God. You will be sinless.

You will be unselfish, strong, and calm.

But people who care

about what their actions will get them are greedy.

They do not do things for God.

They do them for a reward.

Their mood keeps changing.

They are happy one moment and unhappy the next.

They are often angry.

If you do your duty wisely for God's sake alone,

even by killing you do not sin.

ज्ञानं कर्म च कर्ता च त्रिधैव गुणभेदतः ।
प्रोच्यते गुणसंख्याने यथावच्छृणु तान्यपि ॥१९॥
सर्वभूतेषु येनैकं भावमव्ययमीक्षते ।
अविभक्तं विभक्तेषु तज्ज्ञानं विद्धि सात्त्विकम् ॥२०॥
पृथक्त्वेन तु यज्ज्ञानं नानाभावान्पृथग्विधान् ।
वेत्ति सर्वेषु भूतेषु तज्ज्ञानं विद्धि राजसम् ॥२१॥
यत्तु कृत्स्नवदेकस्मिन्कार्ये सक्तमहैतुकम् ।
अतत्त्वार्थवदल्पं च तत्तामसमुदाहृतम् ॥२२॥
नियतं सङ्गरहितमरागद्वेषतः कृतम् ।
अफलप्रेप्सुना कर्म यत्तत्सात्त्विकमुच्यते ॥२३॥

यत्तु कामेप्सुना कर्म साहंकारेण वा पुनः ।
क्रियते बहुलायासं तद्राजसमुदाहृतम् ॥२४॥
अनुबन्धं क्षयं हिंसामनवेक्ष्य च पौरुषम् ।
मोहादारभ्यते कर्म यत्तत्तामसमुच्यते ॥२५॥
मुक्तसङ्गोऽनहंवादी धृत्युत्साहसमन्वितः ।
सिद्ध्यसिद्ध्योर्निर्विकारः कर्ता सात्त्विक उच्यते ॥२६॥
रागी कर्मफलप्रेप्सुर्लुब्धो हिंसात्मकोऽशुचिः ।
हर्षशोकान्वितः कर्ता राजसः परिकीर्तितः ॥२७॥
अयुक्तः प्राकृतः स्तब्धः शठो नैष्कृतिकोऽलसः ।
विषादी दीर्घसूत्री च कर्ता तामस उच्यते ॥२८॥

Oh Arjun,

there are three kinds of action.

The best action is done for God's sake.

Action done for selfishness

or only for pleasure is bad.

The worst is action done out of ignorance

and foolishness.

The worst thing to do is to act without understanding.

Such action hurts others and hurts yourself.

There are also three kinds of knowledge.

The best kind sees God as One in all beings.

Knowledge which thinks that all beings are separate

is lower.

But the worst knowledge

is thinking that beings can exist without God.

Such knowledge is false.

बुद्धेर्भेदं धृतेश्चैव गुणतस्त्रिविधं शृणु ।
प्रोच्यमानमशेषेण पृथक्त्वेन धनंजय ॥२९॥
प्रवृत्तिं च निवृत्तिं च कार्याकार्ये भयाभये ।
बन्धं मोक्षं च या वेत्ति बुद्धिः सा पार्थ सात्त्विकी ॥३०॥
यया धर्ममधर्मं च कार्यं चाकार्यमेव च ।
अयथावत्प्रजानाति बुद्धिः सा पार्थ राजसी ॥३१॥

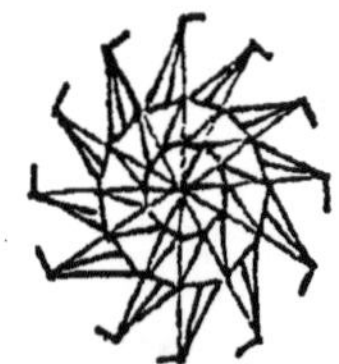

अधर्मं धर्ममिति या मन्यते तमसाऽऽवृता ।
सर्वार्थान् विपरीतांश्च बुद्धिः सा पार्थ तामसी ॥३२॥

धृत्या यया धारयते मनःप्राणेन्द्रियक्रियाः ।
योगेनाव्यभिचारिण्या धृतिः सा पार्थ सात्त्विकी ॥३३॥
यया तु धर्मकामार्थान् धृत्या धारयतेऽर्जुन ।
प्रसङ्गेन फलाकाङ्क्षी धृतिः सा पार्थ राजसी ॥३४॥
यया स्वप्नं भयं शोकं विषादं मदमेव च ।
न विमुञ्चति दुर्मेधा धृतिः सा पार्थ तामसी ॥३५॥

And there are three kinds of reason.
Reason means choosing between right and wrong
and understanding what is good.
The best kind of reason understands
goodness, bravery and freedom.
Reason that mixes up right and wrong is bad.
But the worst reason is sure
that wrong is right and that right is wrong.
It stupidly says that good things are bad
and that bad things are good.
There are also three ways of being firm
and sticking to what you do.
The best way is being firm and steady
about praying and thinking of God.
Another way of being firm is sticking to riches
and to pleasure. That is bad. But the worst way
is sticking to unhappiness, fear and anger.

सुखं त्विदानीं त्रिविधं शृणु मे भरतर्षभ ।
अभ्यासाद्रमते यत्र दुःखान्तं च निगच्छति ॥३६॥

यत्तदग्रे विषमिव परिणामेऽमृतोपमम् ।
तत्सुखं सात्त्विकं प्रोक्तमात्मबुद्धिप्रसादजम् ॥३७॥

विषयेन्द्रियसंयोगाद् यत्तदग्रेऽमृतोपमम् ।
परिणामे विषमिव तत्सुखं राजसं स्मृतम् ॥३८॥

यदग्रे चानुबन्धे च सुखं मोहनमात्मनः ।
निद्रालस्यप्रमादोत्थं तत्तामसमुदाहृतम् ॥३९॥

न तदस्ति पृथिव्यां वा दिवि देवेषु वा पुनः ।
सत्त्वं प्रकृतिजैर्मुक्तं यदेभिः स्यात् त्रिभिर्गुणैः ॥४०॥

Now, Oh brave Arjun,
I will tell you about three kinds of joy.

The best comes from praying and thinking about God.
The second kind of joy is not as good.
It comes from getting the things you like.
And the third kind of joy is bad.
It comes from fooling yourself and from laziness.

At first, praying and thinking quietly of God
seems boring and bitter as poison.
Having fun and getting things you like seems wonderful.
But later, thinking of God,
loving Him, and understanding Him
are wonderful and beautiful.
Then just getting what you want
seems bitter and foolish.

ब्राह्मणक्षत्रियविशां शूद्राणां च परन्तप ।
कर्माणि प्रविभक्तानि स्वभावप्रभवैर्गुणैः ॥४१॥

शमो दमस्तपः शौचं क्षान्तिरार्जवमेव च ।
ज्ञानं विज्ञानमास्तिक्यं ब्रह्मकर्म स्वभावजम् ॥४२॥

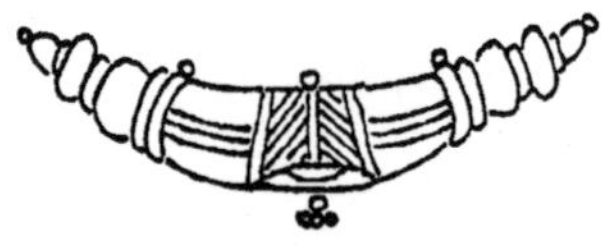

शौर्यं तेजो धृतिर्दाक्ष्यं युद्धे चाप्यपलायनम् ।
दानमीश्वरभावश्च क्षात्रं कर्म स्वभावजम् ॥४३॥

And Arjun,
there are different kinds of duties in life
for different kinds of people.

The Brahmin's duty, for which he is born,
is self control.
The Brahmin's duty is studying holy books
and concentrating on God.
The Brahmin should be peaceful, pure,
forgiving, wise, honest and full of faith in God.

The Kshatriya's duty is to be a soldier.
It is to be a good warrior and a good ruler.
The Kshatriya's nature is to be brave and generous.
His duties fit the Kshatriya's nature.

कृषिगौरक्ष्यवाणिज्यं वैश्यकर्म स्वभावजम् ।
परिचर्यात्मकं कर्म शूद्रस्यापि स्वभावजम् ॥४४॥

स्वे स्वे कर्मण्यभिरतः संसिद्धिं लभते नरः ।
स्वकर्मनिरतः सिद्धिं यथा विन्दति तच्छृणु ॥४५॥

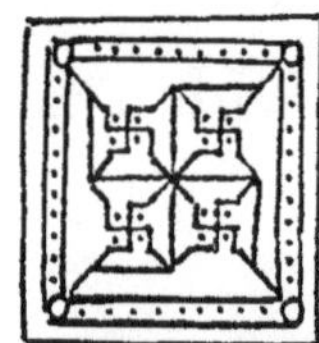

यतः प्रवृत्तिर्भूतानां येन सर्वमिदं ततम् ।
स्वकर्मणा तमभ्यर्च्य सिद्धिं विन्दति मानवः ॥४६॥

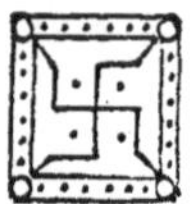

श्रेयान् स्वधर्मो विगुणः परधर्मात्स्वनुष्ठितात् ।
स्वभावनियतं कर्म कुर्वन्नाप्नोति किल्बिषम् ॥४७॥

सहजं कर्म कौन्तेय सदोषमपि न त्यजेत् ।
सर्वारम्भा हि दोषेण धूमेनाग्निरिवावृताः ॥४८॥

The Vaishya's duty is to plant food,
to protect cows and to do business.
These jobs are right for the Vaishya.

The Shudra's duty is doing work for the other groups.
This is his duty for which he is born.

Each and every person can reach God
by doing her own duty well.
Each person can become perfect
simply by doing her duty.
It is better to do your own simple duty
than someone else's greater job.

No one should give up her duty,
whatever it may be.

असक्तबुद्धिः सर्वत्र जितात्मा विगतस्पृहः ।
नैष्कर्म्यसिद्धिं परमां संन्यासेनाधिगच्छति ॥४९॥
सिद्धिं प्राप्तो यथा ब्रह्म तथाऽऽप्नोति निबोध मे ।
समासेनैव कौन्तेय निष्ठा ज्ञानस्य या परा ॥५०॥
बुद्ध्या विशुद्धया युक्तो धृत्यात्मानं नियम्य च ।
शब्दादीन्विषयांस्त्यक्त्वा रागद्वेषौ व्युदस्य च ॥५१॥

विविक्तसेवी लघ्वाशी यतवाक्कायमानसः ।
ध्यानयोगपरो नित्यं वैराग्यं समुपाश्रितः ॥५२॥

अहंकारं बलं दर्पं कामं क्रोधं परिग्रहम् ।
विमुच्य निर्ममः शान्तो ब्रह्मभूयाय कल्पते ॥५३॥
ब्रह्मभूतः प्रसन्नात्मा न शोचति न काङ्क्षति ।
समः सर्वेषु भूतेषु मद्भक्तिं लभते पराम् ॥५४॥
भक्त्या मामभिजानाति यावान्यश्चास्मि तत्त्वतः ।
ततो मां तत्त्वतो ज्ञात्वा विशते तदनन्तरम् ॥५५॥

Now I will tell you
what a perfect person is like.

The perfect person eats lightly and lives quietly.
She controls her mind and keeps it thinking of God.
She controls her body and is calm.
She is part of God.
She and God are joined.
They are One.

The person who is good enough to join God
is not selfish, angry, greedy or proud.

The perfect person is cheerful. She is never sad.
She never wants or needs anything.
By loving God she gets to know God
and becomes part of God.

सर्वकर्माण्यपि सदा कुर्वाणो मद्व्यपाश्रयः ।
मत्प्रसादादवाप्नोति शाश्वतं पदमव्ययम् ॥५६॥

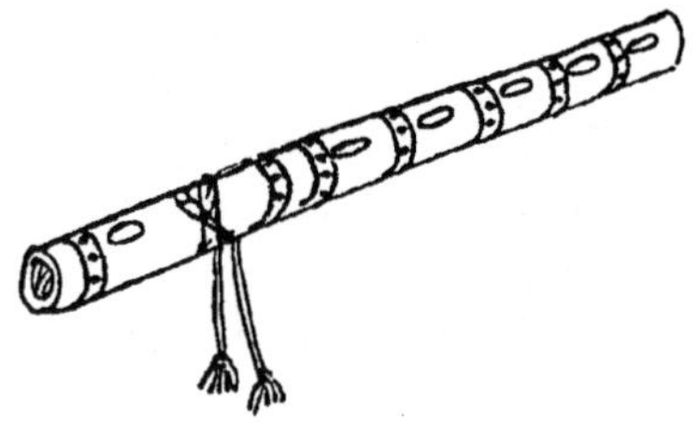

चेतसा सर्वकर्माणि मयि संन्यस्य मत्परः ।
बुद्धियोगमुपाश्रित्य मच्चित्तः सततं भव ॥५७॥

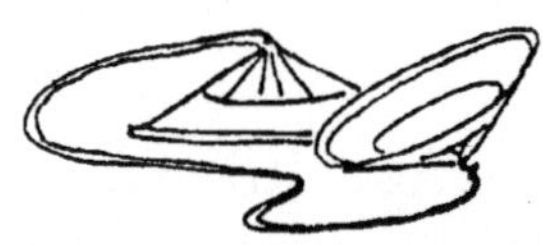

मच्चित्तः सर्वदुर्गाणि मत्प्रसादात्तरिष्यसि ।
अथ चेत्त्वमहंकारान्न श्रोष्यसि विनङ्क्ष्यसि ॥५८॥

The perfect person keeps on doing his duty.

He keeps on doing things.

He does not give up action.

He only gives up the fruit of action.

This means he does everything

for God's sake.

So, you see,

you should do everything for Me.

Give up your actions to Me.

Give yourself up to Me.

Concentrate on Me all the time.

If your mind is always on God,

I will always help you when you need help.

But if you do not listen to Me, you will be destroyed.

You will be completely ruined.

यदहंकारमाश्रित्य न योत्स्य इति मन्यसे ।
मिथ्यैष व्यवसायस्ते प्रकृतिस्त्वां नियोक्ष्यति ॥५९॥

स्वभावजेन कौन्तेय निबद्धः स्वेन कर्मणा ।
कर्तुं नेच्छसि यन्मोहात्करिष्यस्यवशोऽपि तत् ॥६०॥

ईश्वरः सर्वभूतानां हृद्देशेऽर्जुन तिष्ठति ।
भ्रामयन्सर्वभूतानि यन्त्रारूढानि मायया ॥६१॥

तमेव शरणं गच्छ सर्वभावेन भारत ।
तत्प्रसादात्परां शान्तिं स्थानं प्राप्स्यसि शाश्वतम् ॥६२॥

इति ते ज्ञानमाख्यातं गुह्याद्गुह्यतरं मया ।
विमृश्यैतदशेषेण यथेच्छसि तथा कुरु ॥६३॥

सर्वगुह्यतमं गुह्यः शृणु मे परमं वचः ।
इष्टोऽसि मे दृढमिति ततो वक्ष्यामि ते हितम् ॥६४॥

You are proud and silly Arjun,
if you, a Kshatriya, say, "I will not fight."
Fighting is your nature.
It is your duty and your own nature will make you fight.

Oh Arjun, remember
God lives in the hearts of all beings
and makes them act. Trust God.
Go to God for protection and peace.

Oh Arjun, this is My secret.
Now I have given it to you.
Think about it and do whatever you wish.

Arjun, listen again to My final most secret words.
I will tell them to you for your own good
because I love you.

मन्मना भव मद्भक्तो मद्याजी मां नमस्कुरु ।
मामेवैष्यसि सत्यं ते प्रतिजाने प्रियोऽसि मे ॥६५॥

सर्वधर्मान्परित्यज्य मामेकं शरणं व्रज ।
अहं त्वा सर्वपापेभ्यो मोक्षयिष्यामि मा शुचः ॥६६॥

ॐ

इदं ते नातपस्काय नाभक्ताय कदाचन ।
न चाशुश्रूषवे वाच्यं न च मां योऽभ्यसूयति ॥६७॥

ॐ

य इदं परमं गुह्यं मद्भक्तेष्वभिधास्यति ।
भक्तिं मयि परां कृत्वा मामेवैष्यत्यसंशयः ॥६८॥

न च तस्मान्मनुष्येषु कश्चिन्मे प्रियकृत्तमः ।
भविता न च मे तस्मादन्यः प्रियतरो भुवि ॥६९॥

Think of Me, love Me, worship Me,
bow down to Me
and you will surely reach Me.
I promise you.

Give yourself up to Me
and I will forgive all your mistakes.
Do not worry.

My secret should not be told to anyone
who does not love God or to anyone
who does not want to hear it.

But whoever tells it to people who love Me, God,
will be sure to come to Me.

No one is dearer to Me than a person who loves Me.

अध्येष्यते च य इमं धर्म्यं संवादमावयोः ।
ज्ञानयज्ञेन तेनाहमिष्टः स्यामिति मे मतिः ॥७०॥

श्रद्धावाननसूयश्च शृणुयादपि यो नरः ।
सोऽपि मुक्तः शुभाँल्लोकान् प्राप्नुयात्पुण्यकर्मणाम् ॥७१॥

कच्चिदेतच्छ्रुतं पार्थ त्वयैकाग्रेण चेतसा ।
कच्चिदज्ञानसंमोहः प्रनष्टस्ते धनञ्जय ॥७२॥

And whoever has heard or read My words
in this conversation with you, Arjun, loves Me.
Whoever has thought about My words carefully,
worships Me with wisdom.
Whoever understands these words
I have just spoken to you,
is wise.
Whoever has listened, full of faith to My message
will be sure to get goodness and happiness.

And now, Oh Arjun, son of Kunti,
did you keep your mind on everything
I have said to you?
Did you understand My message?
Do you now know the Truth?
Have your confusion
and your unhappiness gone away?

नष्टो मोहः स्मृतिर्लब्धा त्वत्प्रसादान्मयाच्युत ।
स्थितोऽस्मि गतसंदेहः करिष्ये वचनं तव ॥७३॥

इत्यहं वासुदेवस्य पार्थस्य च महात्मनः ।
संवादमिममश्रौषमद् भुतं रोमहर्षणम् ॥७४॥

व्यासप्रसादाच्छ्रुतवानेतद् गुह्यमहं परम् ।
योगं योगेश्वरात्कृष्णात् साक्षात्कथयतः स्वयम् ॥७५॥

राजन्संस्मृत्य संस्मृत्य संवादमिममद्भुतम् ।
केशवार्जुनयोः पुण्यं हृष्यामि च मुहुर्मुहुः ॥७६॥

तच्च संस्मृत्य संस्मृत्य रूपमत्यद्भुतं हरेः ।
विस्मयो मे महान् राजन् हृष्यामि च पुनः पुनः ॥७७॥

Arjun said:

Lord Krishna,

because of Your mercy I know the Truth.

I will be firm and do what You wish.

I will fight!

Sanjay said:

And so I heard the marvelous exciting conversation

between Krishna Bhagvan and Arjun.

Through God's grace I heard this most secret Yoga.

I think, Oh King,

of this wonderful holy conversation and I am happy.

I rejoice again and again.

I keep remembering

how wonderful Lord Krishna looked

and I am happy and delighted again and again.

ॐ

यत्र योगेश्वरः कृष्णो यत्र पार्थो धनुर्धरः ।
तत्र श्रीर्विजयो भूतिर्ध्रुवा नीतिर्मतिर्मम ॥७८॥

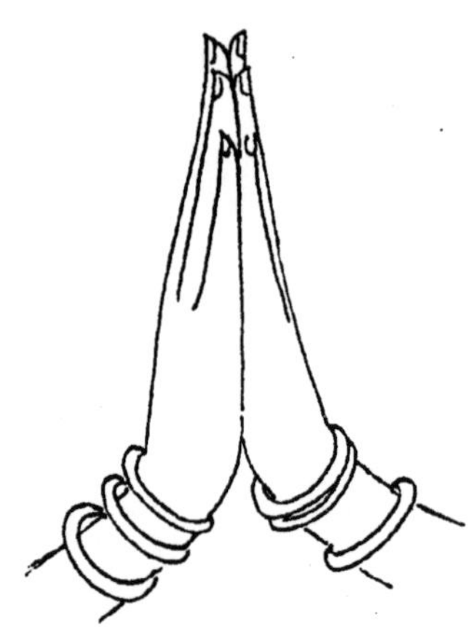

Wherever there is Lord Krishna
and brave Arjun,
there will be happiness, victory,
glory and truth.

OM TAT SAT

Epilogue

Thus the war at Kurukshetra was fought. It lasted eighteen days and on each of these days brave warriors were killed. Young and old heroes fought and died with courage. The great wise Bhishma, Arjun's young son Abhimanyu, the respected Drona, and Karna, son of Kunti and the sun god, fell. Duryodhana was killed by Bhim and even at the moment of death he did not stop hating the Pandavas.

At last the war ended and victory came to the Pandavas. But it was a bitter victory. They went once again back to Hastinapura, their family home, now a city of sadness and emptiness.

Years passed. Yudishtir ruled wisely and kindly. So, gradually the sorrows caused by the terrible war softened.

The Mahabharata War could not have been stopped. Its wheels had been set turning by jealousy, hatred and foolishness. Arjun and his brothers, as Kshatryas, had no honorable choice but to fight courageously.

Arjun understood all that Lord Krishna taught him on the battlefield of Kurukshetra. He finally arose and fought, understanding that it was his duty.

He trusted in God and did everything in his life for God.

Whoever is lucky enough to hear about God's message in the Bhagavad Gita has a chance to understand the truth just like Arjun. Understanding the truth is being wise. Wisdom puts us on the path to God. This path leads to freedom from death and birth, to God Himself, and to everlasting happiness.

Glossary

ASAT	Something not true
ATMAN	The soul which is God
BHAGVAN	God
BRAHMA	God, the creator of the world
BRAHMIN	Someone from a family of priests
CASTE	Family and work group in which people are born
CHAKRA	A wheel or circle
CONCH	A shell
GANGES	A holy river in India
GARUDA	The bird on which Lord Vishnu rides
GHEE	Butter which is cooked until it is clear
GUNAS	The three ways of the body or of matter: Sattva, Rajas, and Tamas
HIMALAYAS	Very tall mountains in India

HOLY FIRE	Fire used to worship God and to get enlightenment
INDRA	The Lord of gods
JANAK	The father of Sita, Rama's wife
KARMA	Action and work and things that happen from actions
KARMAYOGI	Someone who worships God by good deeds
KSHATRIYA	A warrior
KSHETRA	A field or the body
KSHETRAJNA	Someone who understands the body and who knows what is to be known
LOTUS	A flower that grows in ponds or mud
MAYA	Make believe
MEDITATION	Thinking steadily about God and concentrating on Him
OM	A holy word which means God and the universe
PEEPAL TREE	A holy tree
PUJA	A ceremony to worship God
RAJAS	One of the gunas which causes strong feelings
RAMA	One of God's human forms
RUDRA	God of destruction

SANYASI	Someone who has given up everything for God
SAT	True or truth
SATTVA	One of the gunas which is pure and good
SHIVA or SIVA	One of God's human forms
SHUDRA or SUDRA	Someone from a family of workers or servants
TAMAS	One of the gunas which is impure and bad
TUP	Suffering or punishing yourself for God's sake
VAISHYA	Someone from a family of farmers or business people
VASUS	A group of gods
VEDAS	Ancient holy books about the Hindu religion
VISHNU	One of God's human forms
YAMA	The god of death
YOGA	The way to understand God
YOGI	Someone who understands God

Author Biography

Irina Gajjar — linguist, philosopher, scholar, attorney — speaks English, Gujarati, Chinese, Spanish, Portuguese, Romanian and French and has studied Sanskrit in India for ten years.

Irina, born in Bucharest, Romania, grew up in Manhattan, New York. She then attended high school in Mexico City. At seventeen she graduated Magna cum Laude from Mexico City College, now the University of the Americas, with a Bachelor of Arts degree in Romance Languages. Subsequently she obtained a Master of Arts degree in Spanish from Bryn Mawr College, Pennsylvania. She followed that with a Ph.D. in Ancient Indian Studies from Bombay University in India, and a J.D. degree from the University of Texas at Austin. The renowned historian Dr. William McNeill wrote the preface for Irina's doctoral dissertation, published under the title *Ancient Indian Art and the West.*

For *You Know Me*, Irina's husband, Navin Gajjar, created the handwritten Sanskrit text and the traditional Indian art motifs. Although an artist, he holds three degrees including a Master of Science degree in Mechanical Engineering from the Massachusetts Institute of Technology.

When the Gajjars are not travelling, they live in Mazatlan, Mexico where Irina writes and Navin paints.